Herbs & Spices

The Book of
Herbs
& Spices

John & Rosemary Hemphill

OMEGA BOOKS

contents

This edition published 1984 by Omega Books Ltd,
1 West Street, Ware, Hertfordshire, under licence
from the proprietor.

Copyright © RPLA Pty Ltd 1974

ISBN 1 85007 015 6

Printed and bound in Hong Kong by South China Printing Co.

introduction

There are a tremendous number of different kinds of herbs, and broadly, they may be grouped into three main categories which are culinary, scented, and medicinal. Many of them have a dual or triple purpose of course, but for this book we have concentrated on the culinary and scented kinds which most people are able to grow, and would like to have for everyday use in the kitchen, or for making perfumed gifts. Their medicinal use is touched on as interesting historical knowledge, and a few simple remedies are given, such as herb teas for minor ailments. Medicinal herbs and their application is, in our opinion, a separate specialized subject, and detailed information should only be given by experts.

A separate chapter at the back of the book describes the most widely-known and useful spices which are found on nearly all grocer's shelves today. The difference between a herb and a spice is that herbs are the dried leaves of culinary plants, while true spices are aromatic products from various parts of plants, usually grown in hot countries where their flavour is greatest. The part required is collected and dried, and it may be the buds, bark, berries, fruit, or roots.

When planning to grow herbs, choose a place near the kitchen for convenience. They can be grown in a rockery, along a small pathway leading to a sundial or birdbath, or in their own formal garden, with set patterns dividing the beds.

There are many different kinds of containers to use for growing herbs in flats or units. First it must be remembered that herbs are not indoor plants, and will not give their true fragrance without fresh air and some sunshine during the day. If there is no balcony or porch, it is still possible to grow the smaller herbs in troughs or pots on a window sill. Where there is room, a terra cotta 'strawberry jar' with several apertures around the sides as well as the top, making spaces for approximately 5 different herbs, is an excellent idea: select plants with small root systems for this. There is a choice of parsley, chives, chervil, cress, sage, thyme, marjoram, oregano, savory and salad burnet, with bush basil in the top during the summer. There are also troughs on the market and hanging pots in various sizes. The containers must be filled with a fairly rich, light soil mixture, so that the plants will have nourishment as they grow, and yet will be able to drain properly. Never let herbs in pots dry out. They also should be fed occasionally with one of the brands of 'plant pills' which are available; instructions on how to use them are given on the package.

hints on using fresh and dried herbs

Most recipes in this book give measurements for using fresh herbs. However, there are many people who are unable to grow their own, and as fresh herbs are not always available anyway, a general rule to follow is to use *half* the amount of the dried product. Of course this will also depend on the potency of the dried herbs, so test for flavour on the tip of the tongue. Correctly dried herbs always taste stronger than the fresh, as only the watery content has evaporated, leaving a concentration of essential oils. Whole dried leaves, or chopped or crumbled dried leaves are more powerful in fragrance and taste than powdered herbs, which often include ground stalks as well.

Information on harvesting and drying is given for each herb in their separate sections, as their requirements vary.

If growing your own herbs, it is best to gather them as needed for highest nutritive value. If you wish to keep them fresh for a few days, take newly picked, washed sprays, shake off the excess water, wrap in foil or plastic, and store in the refrigerator. Freshly chopped herbs may be kept for about a week in the same way.

For freezing herbs, the most practical way — and the quickest — is to pick fresh sprays, wash them well, remove stalks, then chop finely. Put the chopped herbs into ice-cube trays with just a little water, and freeze. Alternatively, put herb sprigs (without stalks) in a blender with a little water, then chop finely. Freeze in ice-cube trays as before, and remove the blocks as required: they can be dropped straight into hot cooking, and will melt in a few minutes. Use a little less of the frozen herbs than the fresh, as freezing tends to give them a slightly bitter flavour. Most herbs are suitable for this type of treatment except basil, the leaves bruise and discolour very easily in our experience, although there are no such problems when drying the foliage.

Terracotta 'strawberry jar' is an ideal herb container.

points to remember when propagating and cultivating herbs

Cuttings

When taking cuttings from a parent plant, always keep them in water, or wrapped in a damp cloth until ready to put in the sand. Do not let them wilt.

Use coarse river sand for striking cuttings, never use beach sand as it is too fine and probably contains salt.

When preparing cuttings, always pull off leaves with an upward pull, or use secateurs to avoid tearing the bark.

When removing leaves from cuttings, one-third of the foliage should be left on top.

Never push a cutting into the sand, always make a hole first with a knitting needle or skewer slightly thicker than the cutting.

Trim cuttings with a sharp knife or secateurs just below a leaf node, or just above, with hardwood cuttings.

Insert cuttings two-thirds of the way into the sand and try to cover at least 2 leaf nodes, and more if possible.

When cuttings are first put in sand, flood with water so the sand will pack tightly around the cuttings, then keep sand moist at all times.

Rooted cuttings can be taken from the sand and planted directly into the ground, but to obtain best results with a minimum amount of loss, grow them in small separate pots in semi-shade for several weeks first.

Cuttings must be watered every day.

To help cuttings make roots in cool climates, place them in a glass house, or if this is not possible, lay a sheet of glass over a box, making sure the glass is painted with whitewash to prevent the plants being scorched by the sun's rays.

Seeds

When sowing seeds always keep the seed bed, or box, moist at all times, as drying out even for a short period can cause germination to cease.

Put seed box on a level surface, as accidental overwatering or heavy rain can wash the covering soil and seed to one end of the box.

Pots or tubs must be filled to about 1.2 cm (½ inch) from the top to allow for easy watering.

1. Placing tip cuttings of sage in sand, using a dibbler first for easy insertion.

2. The correct method of propagating a number of cuttings in sand.

3A. Tip cuttings of sage with root system after having remained in sand for several weeks.

3B. Potting up rooted sage cutting.

3C. & 3D.   An established rooted cutting ready to plant out.

4. A hardwood cutting of lemon verbena. Notice the cut is made just above a leaf node.

5. A hardwood cutting of lemon verbena being inserted two-thirds of the way into sand.

6. A hardwood lemon verbena cutting with a well-developed root system.

7. Making drills in a prepared seed box prior to sowing seed.

8. & 9. Sowing seed into prepared drills.

10. Covering seed drills with soil which is finely rubbed between palms of the hands.

11. Firming down seed bed with flat piece of stone. A brick, or something similar, can be used.

12. Ornamental pot planted with salad burnet.

13. A trough planted with oregano, parsley, thyme and chives.

Cultivating Herbs

A well drained porous or sandy soil is preferred by nearly all herbs, unless stated otherwise in their sections. They do not like soil enriched with fertilisers and manures, although garden compost is always helpful. If the ground is heavy, dig it well first, and if sour add some lime before planting. Rockeries are excellent places for growing herbs.

A sunny, open situation suits most herbs best. Where this is not so it has been stated.

Cut old growth and dead wood away regularly to give new growth a chance and to improve the appearance of the plant.

Herbs in our experience have remained free from diseases. However, many of them are vulnerable to leaf-eating pests such as slugs, snails, caterpillars and small beetles. Snail bait will look after the slugs and snails, and a routine twice-weekly dusting with Derris Dust (a non-poisonous old remedy) on dampened foliage should take care of the caterpillars and beetles. For those who wish to build up the strength of their gardens so as to try and eradicate all pests, we recommend a comprehensive book on this subject, *Companion Plants* by Helen Philbrick and Richard B. Gregg, published by Stuart and Watkins, London. This book deals with the placing of certain plants near one another — or not, according to their make-up — for compatibility, and as insect repellents.

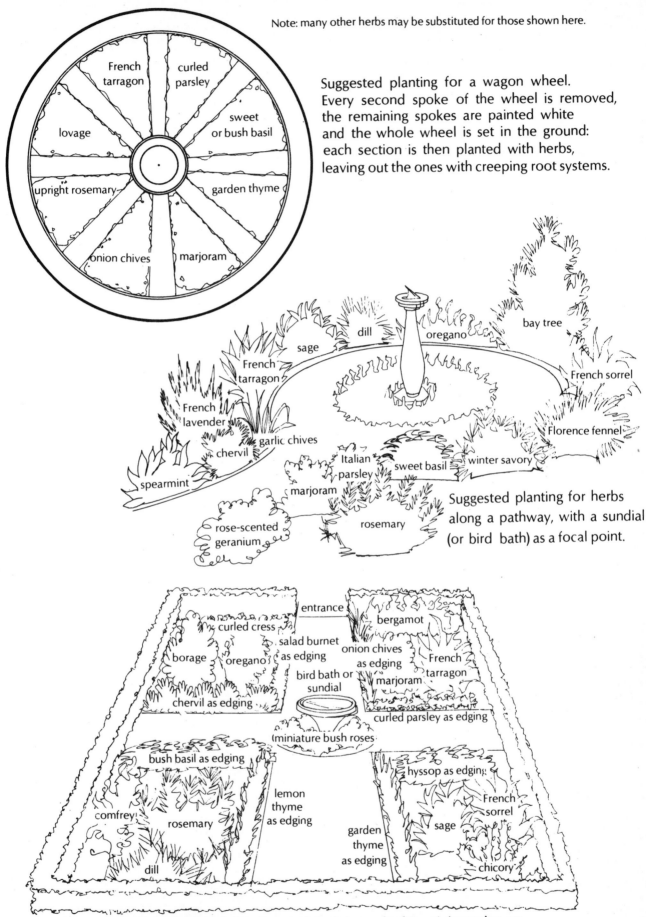

Note: many other herbs may be substituted for those shown here.

French tarragon
curled parsley
sweet or bush basil
lovage
upright rosemary
garden thyme
onion chives
marjoram

Suggested planting for a wagon wheel. Every second spoke of the wheel is removed, the remaining spokes are painted white and the whole wheel is set in the ground: each section is then planted with herbs, leaving out the ones with creeping root systems.

dill
sage
oregano
bay tree
French tarragon
French sorrel
French lavender
garlic chives
chervil
Florence fennel
spearmint
Italian parsley
sweet basil
winter savory
marjoram
rose-scented geranium
rosemary

Suggested planting for herbs along a pathway, with a sundial (or bird bath) as a focal point.

entrance
curled cress
bergamot
borage
oregano
onion chives as edging
French tarragon
salad burnet as edging
marjoram
bird bath or sundial
chervil as edging
curled parsley as edging
miniature bush roses
bush basil as edging
hyssop as edging
comfrey
lemon thyme as edging
French sorrel
rosemary
garden thyme as edging
sage
dill
chicory

A formal herb garden to be enclosed by a hedge of lavender or rosemary; crossed saplings with climbing roses trained over them; a brick or stone wall; or a low picket fence.

angelica

(Angelica archangelica) Umbelliferae. Biennial
Propagation: seeds
Position: shady, sheltered
Soil: rich
Height: 1.50 m-2.40m (5-8 feet)
Part used: seeds, leaves, stalks, roots.

Angelica has serrated bright green leaves, and branching, hollow stems with a celery-like texture; the round, whitish-green flower-heads bloom in November in the second year of growth. When not allowed to flower at all by frequent cutting of the stems, the plant will continue to flourish for several seasons instead of for the customary two years.

Its history goes far back into the legends and folklore of Northern Europe, and in particular the countries of Lapland, Iceland and Russia. Because of Angelica's wonderfully benign qualities, both in the physical and spiritual realms, the plant held an important place in pagan rites, and later in Christian festivals: it was valued as a protection against all sorts of infections; it was used as an aid to digestion, circulation and respiration; and in the cold countries where it was known best, angelica was prized for its ability to give a sensation of warmth when it was eaten.

Many of the old herbalists regarded angelica as the most powerful of all medicinal plants, every part of it — roots, stems, leaves and seeds — having health-giving properties. The subtle aroma which permeates the whole herb is especially delicate, and is yet another reason why angelica is an important ingredient in many beverages, including vermouth and some liqueurs, such as Chartreuse. The earliest liqueurs were prepared in mediaeval monasteries originally as medicines.

When sowing angelica, it is very important to use only fresh seed, as the germinating period is very short. The seed can be sown in prepared boxes, or in the open ground. When seedlings are about 8 cm (3 inches) high, plant out to 90 cm (3 feet) apart in a moist and shady position. Rich soil and some shelter are essential for maximum growth. In poor ground plants will become stunted, and the leaves yellow.

Harvest the seed just before it starts to fall by snipping off and drying whole flower-heads. Sift out any dried husks and stalks, and store seed in airtight containers for household use, but if required for sowing, plant out within a week at the most. The stems can be cut and used at any time; however, their full flavour and size are best just after flowering. The root is stored by digging, washing and keeping in an airy, dry place until needed.

Use: A few young angelica *leaves* may be added to salads; the hollow *stems* and *stalks* can be crystallized and used for decorating sweets and cakes, and if you do not candy your own stems, they can be bought in many shops; the *stems* and *stalks*, either candied or fresh, give flavour and goodness to stewed fruit and milk puddings; a tea can be made from either the *leaves*, *stems*, *seeds*, or the *dried root*. One old remedy for flatulence directs that the *stalks* be slowly chewed until the condition is relieved.

Angelica ice cream

Serves: 4

**2 tablespoons candied angelica,
   chopped
2 tablespoons icing sugar
1 cup whipped cream
2 egg whites, stiffly beaten**

Stir angelica and sugar into the cream, then fold in the egg whites. Turn into ice cream tray and freeze. Serve with vanilla wafers.

15

anise

(Pimpinella anisum) Umbelliferae. Annual
Propagation: seeds
Position: sheltered, sunny
Soil: light, well-drained
Height: 45 cm-60 cm (1½-2 feet)
Part used: seeds, foliage sometimes

Anise has feathery leaves and flat, white flower-heads which bloom in late summer. Aromatic, small, brown seeds or fruit, follow, with a strong licorice taste, most of them having a distinguishing fine hair at one end. The seed is the most useful part of the plant.

Anise is native to the Middle East, and was known in ancient Egypt. Its usefulness as a fragrant and health-giving herb spread to Greece and Rome, and then to many other countries. The Romans discovered that the seeds of anise, and other aromatic spices, helped the digestion after large banquets, so these spices were incorporated into a special cake which was served at the end of a large meal, and is said to be the origin of our special-occasion spicy fruit cakes.

There is another anise called star anise which comes from a tree, *Illicium anisatum*, that is indigenous to China. The oil from these seeds is the same in composition as the annual anise, and equally effective medicinally.

This herb, because of its spindly nature, needs protection from prevailing winds, with plenty of sunshine at the same time to promote healthy growth. The seedlings are soft and fragile and do not transplant well, so it is best to sow directly into the ground. Make sure that the soil is well broken up and in fine seed-bed condition, adding a little lime if the ground is very acid. Unless the soil is extremely poor, fertilizer is not necessary. Sow seeds in September and March in 12 mm (½ inch) deep drills, 30 cm (12 inches) apart. Cover and pack the soil down well, then keep moist until the seedlings appear.

Water regularly in hot, dry weather, preferably in the late afternoon or evening so as not to scorch the plants.

Harvesting the fruit when ripe is simple. After the flower-umbels have become heavy with full, brown seeds, cut the heads off before they drop, store in cardboard boxes, or on sheets of paper, in a dry place, exposing them to direct sunlight when possible to completely dry out any moisture.

Sun-drying is not good for herb leaves, but is helpful in the drying of seed-heads. When crisp and dry, rub the seeds between the palms of the hands. The husk and old flower-heads are easily removed by sifting seeds through a sieve. Store in labelled airtight containers. For culinary use, the seed will last for many years, but for propagating, germination will be more successful if seeds are sown the following season.

Use: *Aniseed* makes the breath sweeter, and is used in the making of cough lozenges; it also flavours some cordials and liqueurs, such as Anisette. A little powdered *seed* added to food for young children will help their digestion, and when some *aniseed* tea is mixed with warm milk and honey, it helps soothe a fretful child. Whole or ground *aniseed* flavours and helps digest many different types of food, such as breads, pasta, cakes and biscuits; stewed or baked apples and pears; vegetables which can be indigestible for many, like cabbages, onions, cucumbers, carrots, turnips and beetroot; and some rich cheese dishes. Anise *leaves* are sometimes used in food — they give a piquant touch to salads; they may also be added to broths and soups while cooking.

Aniseed shortbread biscuits

Makes about 18 medium-sized biscuits

**250 g (8 oz) butter, or vegetable
  margarine
1 cup raw sugar
3 cups self-raising flour, sifted
2 teaspoons aniseed**

Melt the butter in a saucepan, stir in the sugar and flour, then turn mixture into a shallow baking dish which has been rubbed with butter. Push the mixture into the corners and smooth the top with a wooden spoon, then sprinkle with aniseed. Bake in a moderate oven 180ºC (350ºF) for about 30 minutes. Cut the shortbread into squares and leave to cool in the dish.

Aniseed tea

Serves: 1 cup

Measure 1½ cups water into a saucepan and bring to the boil. Add 1 teaspoon aniseed, put on the lid, lower heat and simmer for 15 minutes. Strain and drink hot or warm. (The liquid reduces during simmering.) Sweeten with honey if wished. A little hot milk may also be added to this tea.
For the ground seed, pour 1 cup of boiling water onto ½ teaspoon of anise, then strain through a fine coffee strainer. Drink in the same way.

Fresh herbs: *Hanging l to r* — Florence fennel, oregano, French tarragon, spearmint, thyme, rosemary, sage. *On chopping block* — curled parsley. *On table l to r* — bay leaves, borage leaves and flowers.

Balm

(*Melissa officinalis*) Labiatea. Perennial
Propagation: seeds, cuttings, root division
Position: part sun
Soil: moist, rich
Height: 75 cm (2½ feet)
Part used: leaves

The strong lemon-scented foliage of this herb gives it the popular name of 'lemon balm'. The leaves are crinkly and shaped like mint leaves, although larger in size. The small, white flowers, which bloom in summer, grow in clusters along a thin, angular stem. The plant has a spreading habit, and the shallow roots are thick and matted.

Balm is native to the mountainous regions of Southern Europe, it's botanical name *Melissa* is Latin for 'bee', as these insects are constant visitors to the nectar-laden blossoms when they are in flower. (How wondrously mysterious is the world of nature, for it has been shown that when wax is poured into the honeyed flowers of the Labiatae family, which includes amongst its members thyme, sage, and balm, the hardened shape that results is identical with the bee's proboscis, the organ it uses for extracting honey.) The name of balm has been abbreviated from the fragrant oil balsam, signifying the herb's aromatic sweetness. The leaves contain

Gooseberry and Balm Sherbet (see recipe on page 23).

essences which were highly valued for their healing properties, and were used in treating many ailments such as melancholy, nervous headache, neuralgia and fevers. (Balm tea is still taken today to help bring down high temperatures, and to lessen the effects of exhaustion in hot weather.) Along with sage, it was said to contribute to longevity.

Bee hives were traditionally rubbed with sweet-smelling herbs, especially balm leaves to help keep the hive together and to attract homing bees. Honey was regarded as a necessary commodity for the household larders of bygone days, and there was much written about the art of bee-keeping, those who lived close to these industrious insects having a great respect for their wisdom. Herb gardens and bee hives were traditionally linked together, and Thomas Hyll writes in 1579 that the hives should be placed near: '. . . the hearbe Baulme . . . and manye other sweete and wholesome floures.'

The simplest way to propagate balm is by root division in September, just as the new growth is starting. If you prefer to propagate by taking cuttings, wait for the new tips to grow about 8 cm (3 inches) long, and when firm enough, take a 10 cm (4 inch) long tip, removing all the leaves except the top two; press the cuttings deeply into a pot of river sand, leaving one third of each cutting exposed. Sow seed in September or March into a prepared box, or in shallow drills straight into the ground, leaving a few inches between plants. If seeds are sown fairly thickly, or seedlings are planted close together over an area of several feet, a large clump will develop quickly.

In certain areas the leaves of balm seedlings can get frost-bitten: under these conditions, plant in a sheltered position where there will be some sun during the day. If grown in too wet and shady a place, fungus may give some trouble. Lastly, watch carefully for leaf-eating grubs and insects, and if this occurs, sprinkle the dampened foliage with derris dust.
When using lemon balm fresh, cut the leaves at any time; when drying for storing purposes, cut the stalks back almost to ground level just as the flowers begin to appear, and dry in a shady, airy place; when 'crisp dry' rub leaves from stalks and keep in airtight containers.

Use: The fresh or dried leaves go well in fruit salads, milk puddings, and certain soups and vegetables. Fresh sprigs go into wine cups and cool drinks. A tea can be made from the fresh or dried leaves. Dried balm leaves in pot-pourri give it a delicious lemon scent.

Gooseberry and balm sherbet

(See photograph on page 20)

Serves: 4

> 1 x 155 g (16 oz) can gooseberries
> 150 ml (¼ pint) cream
> 1 tablespoon boiling water
> 1 tablespoon gelatine
> 1 tablespoon chopped balm
> 4 balm sprigs

Place gooseberries and syrup in an electric blender with cream. Pour boiling water onto gelatine, stir until clear, add to other ingredients in blender. Purée together until pulverized and pour into a mixing bowl, fold in the chopped balm. Chill in refrigerator until set. Or press gooseberries and syrup through a sieve, add dissolved gelatine and chopped balm, chill. Serve in cold sherbet glasses with whipped cream, topped with a sprig of balm.

Balm ambrosia

Serves: 6

> ½ cup sugar
> 3 cups water
> several sprigs of balm
> 3 oranges
> 1 lemon
> 4 cups canned pineapple juice

Put the sugar, water and balm into a saucepan and simmer for 5 minutes so that the sugar dissolves and the fragrance is extracted from the balm. Strain into a jug, discarding the balm. Place a few long, fresh sprays of balm into the jug and chill.

Lemon and balm beverage

This lemon and balm beverage, if taken frequently, is particularly helpful for easing a heavy cold.

Makes: 6 cups

Cut up 2 whole lemons, skin and all, and put in a jug with a small bunch of fresh balm (or 2 teaspoons of dried balm). Pour 6 cups of boiling water into the jug and cover. When cool, strain, pressing out as much juice as possible from the lemons and the balm, and stir in 1 tablespoon of honey, or more according to taste. Drink hot or cold throughout the day, a cupful at a time.

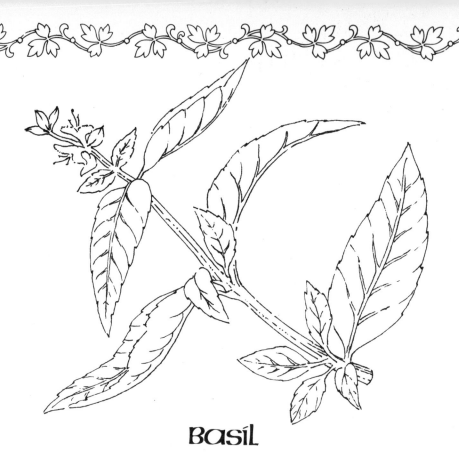

Basil

Basil, Sweet: *(Ocimum basilicum)*
   Labiatae. Annual
Basil, Bush: *(O. minimum)* Labiatae.
   Annual
Propagation: seeds
Position: sunny, sheltered
Soil: light to sandy, well drained
Height: sweet basil, 75 cm (2½ feet);
   bush basil, 30 cm (12 inches)
Part used: leaves

The tender foliage of basil is bright green, with a spicy clove-like aroma. Sweet basil leaves have a stronger perfume than the leaves of bush basil, which are also much smaller. Both varieties have small, white lipped flowers in the autumn.
There is an ornamental, colourful basil, *(O. basilicum purpureum)* which is a variety of sweet basil with rich, purple leaves and pale pink flowers. It is an attractive garden plant and is highly perfumed, but the actual flavour is rank, and it is not recommended for cooking purposes.

Basil originated in India where it was regarded as a sacred herb. It was also known in ancient Egypt, Greece and Rome, and there are many different legends concerning it; the unique and pronounced fragrance it releases into the surrounding atmosphere must have caused much speculation as to the plant's attributes among the wise ancients, who were close to the elemental world. Basil's botanical name of *basilicum* has kingly associations, one early writer saying that the smell was so excellent, that it was 'fit for a king's house'. On the other hand, some say that the name was derived from *basilisk*, a mythical serpent-like creature that could kill with a look, and for many years the plant was linked with poison and 'venomous beasts', while at the same time an application of the herb was prescribed to draw out the poison from stings and bites. One writer's interpretation for basil's old connection with poison as applied to present-day life, is that it will counteract much that is not wholesome in today's food. Like so many other herbs, basil aids digestion, and a tea made from the leaves is said to allay nausea. Once the dried leaves were made into snuff to remedy headaches and colds.

As basil must have warm conditions, early spring sowing is not advised, November being the ideal month in an average climate. Sow the seed directly into the ground in shallow drills, and if the soil is sour, lime it well two weeks before planting, making sure that the bed is well broken up and as fine as possible. If the soil is heavy, a small quantity of river sand will help to make the ground more suitable, both for sowing and drainage. When sweet basil is 8 cm (3 inches) high, thin out to 30 cm (12 inches) between plants. For bush basil, a distance of 15 cm (6 inches) between seedlings is sufficient. As the plants grow it is important to pinch out the centres to ensure a spreading, bushy habit.

When cultivating basil in pots, the most suitable variety to have is bush basil, as it is more compact. An 18 cm (7 inch) pot is an excellent size for this: fill the container with potting soil, and sow 3 to 4 seeds in it, water well and keep moist to ensure germination and satisfactory growth. When seedlings are 8 cm (3 inches) high, choose the sturdiest-looking one to leave in the pot, then prick out the rest, which may be planted into other containers or into the open ground. Remember that basil (or any other herb) will not grow as an indoor plant; a sunny terrace, or a window sill where there is sunshine and fresh air, is the ideal position.

Both basils are susceptible to cold weather, and are very frost-tender as well: even a cold change will kill them, although there may be no frost. It is necessary to harvest basil in March before the cold turns the leaves limp and yellow. (In hot climates basil will grow throughout the year, and under these conditions the seeds will self-sow readily.) For fullest flavour, cut long, leafy stalks for drying just before the plant comes into flower, spreading them out in a shady place on wire mesh to encourage quick drying. Do not hang in bunches as the soft foliage will then dry too slowly and may possibly spoil. Oven drying is not satisfactory, as the leaves, which bruise so easily, are liable to scorch.

Use: Basil's mouth-watering aroma makes it a versatile herb to use in many different types of food. It has a special affinity with tomatoes, and tomato-based dishes, and is excellent with eggplant, zucchini, marrow, squash, and spinach. Added during the last half hour of cooking, it gives zest to pea soup and lentil soup; it is delicious with cream cheese in sandwiches; gives a lift to green salads and sliced cucumbers; is excellent in all pasta dishes (steaming hot spaghetti tossed in oil, with salt and freshly ground pepper and a handful of freshly chopped or dried basil, makes a simple and tasty meal.) It also goes well with poultry, veal, liver, kidneys, fish and shellfish, and makes a savoury vinegar when the leaves are steeped in it for a few weeks.

Salmon and basil loaf
(See photograph on page 38)

Serves: 5—6
Cooking time: 45 minutes
Oven temperature: 180°C (350°F)

> 2 x 440 g cans red salmon, flaked
> 1 cup dry breadcrumbs
> 4 tablespoons tomato paste
> 1 green pepper, finely chopped
> 1 onion, finely chopped
> ½ teaspoon salt
> 1 tablespoon finely chopped basil
> 4 eggs, beaten
> 3 tablespoons vegetable oil

Mash all the ingredients, except the oil, together in a bowl in the order given above. Grease a loaf tin and pack the mixture into it, then refrigerate for a few hours. Loosen the edges with a knife, turn the loaf into a shallow ovenproof dish, and pour the oil over it. Bake in a moderate oven 180°C (350°F) for 45 minutes. Serve hot with the following sauce.

Tomato sauce: Stew 4 medium sized peeled tomatoes in a little butter with salt, pepper and a pinch of sugar and some basil, then thicken with a tablespoon of cornflour smoothed in a little milk. Serve hot in a jug separately.

Spinach and basil tart

(See photograph on page 37)
Ideal dish for lunch or light supper

Serves: 5-6
Cooking time: 45-50 minutes
Oven temperature: 180°C (350°F)

Pastry:
3 cups plain flour
1 teaspoon salt
2-3 tablespoons iced water
3 tablespoons butter, or
vegetable margarine

Filling:
2 packages frozen chopped spinach
1 small can anchovy fillets
6 tablespoons milk
1 tablespoon chopped basil
salt and pepper
1 tomato, sliced thinly
3 eggs
a few capers or sliced olives
ground nutmeg

Pastry: Sift flour and salt together, then rub in the butter until the mixture resembles breadcrumbs. Add water gradually to make a stiff dough, then roll out thinly. Take a buttered 25.5 cm (10 inch) tart plate and line it with the pastry, trimming the edges and pricking it all over with a fork. Put in a moderate oven 180°C (350°F) for 15-20 minutes, or until just cooked.

Filling: Thaw the spinach as instructed on the package. Beat eggs with milk, fold into spinach with the basil, add salt and pepper to taste, and pour into the pastry shell. Make a pattern with anchovies, tomato slices and capers, finish with nutmeg and put back into the oven 180°C (350°F) for a further 30 minutes, or until the filling is firm. Decorate the centre with a fresh basil sprig if available. Serve the tart hot or cold.

Bay tree

(Laurus nobilis) Lauraceae. Perennial
Propagation: seeds, cuttings
Position: sunny, open
Soil: good quality
Height: 12 m (40 feet)
Part used: leaves

The bay is a very large, attractive tree thickly covered with glossy, dark green leaves, which are narrow and approximately 10 cm (4 inches) long; when broken they give off a warmly pungent aroma. Bay trees make excellent tub specimens, especially if grown as standards when the lower branching stems are cut off, and the tops are pruned into rounded shapes: in Europe and America they are often grown in this way, either in gardens, or on each side of a doorway, particularly in front of hotels and clubs.

The bay tree is native to the shores of the Mediterranean, and among its popular names are 'sweet bay', 'bay laurel', 'Roman laurel', 'noble laurel', and 'true laurel'. There is another type of laurel, the cherry laurel *(Prunus laurocerasus)*, which is poisonous and must not be confused with the bay tree.

In spring, the tight, white flower-buds burst into waxy, cream blossoms with pronounced yellow stamens; when in flower, the tree is continually visited by swarms of bees.

When looking at this tree growing in our gardens, or when using the leaves in cooking, it is interesting to think about the old traditions and history associated with the bay. In early Greece and Rome, the greatest honour for those who were victorious on the battlefield, and in the sports arena, was to be crowned with a bay laurel wreath—as were outstanding men of letters too, hence the title of 'poet laureate'. The bay laurel was a part of pagan temple rites and ceremonies, but it also had an important place in early medicine. Externally, an oil from the leaves and berries was applied to bruises and sprains, the oil was also dropped into the ears to relieve pain, and was given in treating rheumatism, hysteria and flatulence. The powdered berries were sometimes prescribed to improve the appetite and cure fevers.

To propagate bay trees, cuttings are advised, as the seeds do not germinate readily: the seeds are about the size of a pea and are very hard, like a nut. It is necessary to sow them at least 25 mm (1 inch) below the soil's surface; do not be disappointed if there is only about five percent germination. Cuttings are taken when the new spring leaves have hardened, say in November. Each cutting should be 15 cm (6 inches) long, and of new wood. Break the cutting away from the old wood leaving a heel 6 mm (¼ inch) long, which must be trimmed carefully with a sharp knife to eliminate any bark which overhangs the heel. Strip the bottom leaves off the cutting, leaving two-thirds of bare stalk to press into a pot of wet river sand, firming it in with the fingers. Keep cuttings watered at all times; by the end of May they should have made roots, and will be ready to plant out into containers holding potting mixture. (For slow-growing plants such as bay trees, it is always advisable to establish them in pots for at least a year, rather than putting them straight into the garden.)

Bay trees are very susceptible to white wax scale, which makes the foliage sooty and unattractive, and causes poor leaf growth as well: this can be controlled by spraying with white oil in hot weather, or scrubbing the affected places with soapy water.

The leaves can be used for cooking at any time during the year. If wishing to dry them, the best way is to pick the leaves off the stalks, then spread them out on a wire rack, where they will dry quickly with a good green colour. An alternative is to hang leafy branches in bunches in a dark airy place.

Use: Today, we find that bay leaves are indispensable in many different types of cooking, for instance a bay leaf is an essential ingredient in a 'bouquet garni', the other herbs being a spray each of parsley, marjoram and thyme — these are tied together and dropped into casseroles, soups, or stews, and removed after cooking. Or, the dried herbs, including the bay, may be crushed and crumbled together to make a blend, which is then put straight into the pot and left to amalgamate into the stock during cooking. Bay leaves on their own flavour soups and casseroles; boiled, baked or steamed fish, meat and poultry; a bay leaf gives a pungent aroma to marinades, and if a leaf is placed on top of a milk pudding as it goes into the oven, a subtle and unusual flavour is imparted.

Thick oxtail and lentil stew

This is a tasty and nourishing cold weather dish.

Serves: 6
Cooking time: 3 hours

> **2 cut oxtails**
> **2 tablespoons flour**
> **2 tablespoons vegetable oil**
> **6 cups water**
> **½ teaspoon each peppercorns and
>   juniper berries**
> **2 bay leaves**
> **a branch of garden thyme**
> **2 cloves of garlic, chopped**
> **½ cup green lentils**
> **3 teaspoons salt**
> **1 large carrot, chopped**
> **1 small turnip, chopped**
> **2 onions, chopped**
> **2 stalks celery, chopped**
> **parsley for garnish**

Roll oxtails in flour, then brown all over in a saucepan in the oil. Add water and bring to the boil with the lid on. Add peppercorns, juniper berries, bay leaves, thyme, garlic, lentils and salt. Lower heat, cover and simmer for 2 hours, skimming off the fat as it rises to the surface. Add all the vegetables and simmer for another hour. Sprinkle chopped parsley over each helping. Serve with steaming-hot boiled potatoes.

Bergamot

(Monarda didyma) Labiatea. Perennial
Propagation: seeds, root division
Position: shady, morning sun
Soil: rich, moist
Height: 1.20 m (4 feet)
Part used: leaves, flowers

The flowers of bergamot, in size, colour and form, are amongst the showiest of all herb blossoms. There are several different colours, varying in hue from pink and mauve to a rich red, which is the popular Cambridge Scarlet. Bergamot's slightly hairy leaves are oval — approximately 8 cm (3 inches) long, and are attached in pairs to square stems. The pom-pom type flowers start blooming on tall 90 cm (3 feet) high stalks in early summer, and if plants are in the right position where the roots are shaded, and where there is morning sun for several hours, you will have flowers right through to mid-autumn. The whole plant is fragrantly scented, and the tubular flower petals are full of nectar, making them a magnet for bees; for this reason bergamot is often called 'bee balm'. Honey-eating birds are also attracted to the blossoms. Like mint, which is a member of the same family, bergamot has a matted, spreading root system, and does not start shooting upwards until spring. A dressing of well-decayed humus may be applied at this time, and grass cuttings should be sprinkled over the roots during the hottest part of summer.

Bergamot is native to North America, and received its botanical name from the sixteenth century Spanish physician, Nicholas Monardez, who first discovered and described it. The leaves, which contain the essential oil thymol, were widely used in an infusion by the Oswego Indians. The herb soon became known to the early American settlers, who called it Oswego Tea, a name which is still popular today. The tea, as well as being a pleasant beverage, is a remedy for sore throats, colds and chest complaints.

Oil of bergamot, a fragrant essence, does not come from this plant, but from a citrus tree, the bergamot orange, *(Citrus bergamia)*. The aromas are similar.

Bergamot may be grown in clumps as background plants in herb gardens, or in decorative clusters in standard garden beds, the lovely, plush-red, pin-cushion blooms making splashes of vivid colour. Ours grows in a far-away bed set in a green sward surrounded by a glade of leafy trees: when in bloom, the scarlet flashes draw one from a distance to investigate and admire; a flower is always picked and the honeysuckle-petals tasted for their sweetness. If necessary, lightly tie the slender and rather brittle stems to garden stakes.

Propagation by root division can be done throughout the year; however, the best time is in September when new growth is beginning. The seeds, which are very small, can be sown in a prepared box in September, and planted out when big enough to handle, leaving 15 cm (6 inches) between plants. The fact that bergamot likes to grow in a shady position where the roots can be kept cool and moist, also encourages snails, so be prepared for this by laying a suitable bait nearby, especially when the soft leaves are young. After the plants have finished flowering, cut all stalks back to ground level.

For drying, harvest both foliage and flowers in late summer when the plant is in full bloom, and dry as quickly as possible. Do this by picking the leaves and blooms from the stems, and spreading them out on a wire rack in a shady place: when dry, store them in airtight containers.

Use: Bergamot *leaves* go into salads, teas, and cooling summer beverages; their savoury, yet fruity aroma enhances such widely differing foods as vegetable dishes, and sweet jellies; they combine well with pork and veal; fresh or dried, they may be used instead of mint leaves for a change; they make an excellent and fragrant addition to pot-pourri. The *flowers* can be gently torn apart and added to a tossed green salad, and when dried, they add colour and perfume to pot-pourri.

32

Tomato and bergamot loaf
(Elizabeth's recipe)

Serves: 4
Cooking time: 20 minutes
Oven temperature: 180°C (350°F)

1½ cups canned tomatoes with juice
2 tablespoons water
2 tablespoons chopped bergamot
  leaves
1 cup celery, chopped
1½ cups package breadcrumbs
1 cup grated tasty cheese
2 tablespoons vegetable oil
2 tablespoons onion, grated
½ teaspoon salt
2 eggs, beaten

Break up tomatoes and mix together with all the ingredients in the order given, spoon into an oiled ovenproof dish and bake in a moderate oven 180°C (350°F) for 20 minutes. Serve hot.

Port wine and bergamot jelly
(See photograph on page 55)

Serves: 4

3 rounded teaspoons gelatine
½ cup hot water
2 tablespoons clear honey
2 tablespoons lemon juice
1 cup port wine
1 tablespoon finely chopped
  bergamot (or spearmint)

Dissolve gelatine in hot water, stir in the rest of the ingredients in the order given. Pour into a tray and freeze. When ready to serve, roughly fork through the jelly to give it a frosty look, spoon into glasses and top with ice-cream or cream. Decorate each serving with a sprig of bergamot, or the red, honeyed petals of bergamot flowers.

Borage

(Borago officinalis) Boraginaceae.
 Annual
Propagation: seeds
Position: semi-shade, sheltered
Soil: light, moist
Height: 90 cm (3 feet)
Part used: leaves, flowers

This herb has thick, soft stems and large leaves, both of which are covered in fine, bristly hairs: the leaves when fully grown are approximately 23 cm (9 inches) long, and 15 cm (6 inches) wide, the flowers are star-shaped and a vivid sky-blue, with an occasional pale pink bloom appearing amongst the blue. There is also a rare species with white flowers. The blooms are filled with nectar, making them an excellent source of food for bees.

Borage first came from the Middle East, old chronicles saying that Aleppo was its original home. Throughout the ages, wherever it was taken, this plant has spread abundantly, adapting well to almost any soil and climate. The branching, leafy plants are rich in potassium, calcium, mineral acids, and a very beneficial saline mucilage.

Borage leaves and flowers were an important ingredient in wine cups and other beverages to 'make men and women merry and glad'. The cucumber-flavoured leaves were eaten to help cleanse the blood, and were especially recommended for convalescents; borage sprigs in the diet were said to 'cheer the hard student'; and the foliage was used extensively as a pot-herb, as it still is.

The flowers are potent, too, and these were put into salads for 'gladness'; syrups were made from them to help cure fevers and jaundice; when made into sugary conserves they were prescribed for weakness and faintings — a delectable medicine which would not have been hard to swallow! The flowers, with their prominent black anthers and five-pointed petals of brilliant blue, were also favourite subjects in the needlework of past centuries, partly for their simple beauty, and for their association with bravery and courage.

Borage seed germinates so easily that it can be sown in all seasons in mild climates. In very cold areas, the best time for cultivating is in September, when the oblong, black seeds can be sown into the open ground into shallow drills, 30 cm (1 foot) apart, making sure that the ground has been well turned over first, so that the soil is reasonably fine. The position for growing the plants should be moist, with not too much sun: there should also be shelter from winds as the main stems, being soft, are easily broken. Borage is in bloom nearly all through the year, and is continually seeding itself, so that once planted, you should never be without it. It seems to do best when allowed to grow in thick clumps, the plants help to support each other, and the massed effect of the misty buds and blue flowers is pleasing. If on the other hand, borage begins to take over the garden, it is easily thinned out and the shallow roots dislodged — even when fully grown — by pulling out the stems by hand, remembering that the stalks are prickly.

Borage leaves and flowers may be used fresh at any time of the year. Drying the leaves and flowers is possible, but the method must be quick to prevent spoilage. Take the flowers and leaves off the stalks and place them on wire racks in a shady, airy place. When dry, store in airtight containers.

Use: The young *leaves* can be very finely chopped, almost minced, and mixed into green salads, or used as fillings, with a little salt and pepper, for sandwiches; whole young *leaves* go into punches and wine cups, or they can be dipped in batter, fried, and eaten as a vegetable; older *leaves* can be used for soup, these should be finely chopped too; fresh or dried *leaves* make a health-giving tea. The blue *flowers* can be floated on top of all kinds of drinks, and scattered over a green salad just before serving; when crystallized they decorate cream-swirled sweets and iced cakes; the fresh or dried *flowers* make a tea.

Green dandelion and borage salad

Dandelion leaves are a natural health food. They are a blood cleanser, and are beneficial to the liver, gall-bladder, kidneys and digestion. It is best to use the tender young leaves.

Serves: 4-6

> **8 young dandelion leaves, washed and dried**
> **½ lettuce, washed and dried**
> **1 tablespoon each finely chopped borage leaves and chives**
> **½ thin-skinned orange, unpeeled and finely sliced**
> **4 tablespoons vegetable oil**
> **1 tablespoon white vinegar or lemon juice**
> **1 clove garlic, finely chopped**
> **1 teaspoon salt**
> **pepper**

Tear dandelion and lettuce leaves into a salad bowl, add borage leaves, chives, and orange. Blend oil, vinegar, garlic, salt and pepper together and toss through the salad. Scatter the borage flowers over the top and serve.

Blender borage soup
(See photograph on page 56)

Serves: 4-6

> **1 cup mashed potato (may be made with instant potato)**
> **1 bunch, or 125 g (4 oz) borage leaves, washed and roughly chopped**
> **½ teaspoon salt**
> **4 cups chicken stock (may be made with 2 chicken cubes)**

Put potato, borage leaves and salt into blender with as much stock as will fit into it. Turn onto high for a few seconds, or until borage is finely chopped and soup is blended. Pour into a saucepan and stir in the rest of the stock, adding more salt if necessary. Heat and serve. In summer this soup is delicious chilled and served cold.

Preparation for Spinach and Basil Tart (see recipe on page 27).

caraway

(Carum carvi) Umbelliferae. Biennial
Propagation: seeds
Position: sheltered, sunny
Soil: average, well drained
Height: 60 cm (2 feet)
Part used: seeds, roots, fresh leaves
    sometimes

Caraway plants grow to 60 cm (2 feet) high, their foliage is delicate, finely-cut and frond-like, and their white umbrella-like flowers bloom in summer. These flowers are followed by seeds, or fruit, which are brown and crescent-shaped, and are marked with distinctive ridges. The roots are thick and tapering, and are similar in appearance to a small parsnip.

Caraway is indigenous to all parts of Europe and is also claimed to be native to parts of Asia, India, and North Africa. Its therapeutic and useful qualities as a medicine and in food were known as far back as Biblical times, the ancient Arabs having called the seeds *Karawya*.

Caraway seeds can be sown in September, and where the climate is mild, in March as well. Choose a sunny, sheltered position in the garden and sow the seed into shallow drills, 20 cm (8 inches) apart. When plants are about 8 cm (3 inches) high, thin them out to a distance of 15 cm (6 inches). As the

Salmon and Basil Loaf with Tomato Sauce (see recipe on page 26); Beans and Savory (see recipe on page 92); Baked Tomatoes with Mint (see recipe on page 78).

seedlings do not transplant well, it is not advisable to start them in seed boxes.

For harvesting, when the seeds are about to drop, cut off all the heads, and like anise flowers, dry on sheets of paper in a shady place, exposing them to the sun when possible. They are ready to store when the fruit falls away easily from the shrivelled flower-heads if given a light shake. Sieve out any pieces of stalk, and pack into airtight containers. If using the roots for culinary purposes, they should be pulled when young, and if this is a favourite way to use your caraway, it is a good. idea to make two sowings, one for the root crop and the other for the seeds.

Use: The *seeds* go with boiled or baked onions during cooking, and into potato dishes; sprinkle them into the pot when steaming turnips, beetroot, parsnips, carrots, cabbage and cauliflower; blend them into cream cheese; mix them into home-made breads, biscuits, and cakes; shake a few *seeds* over apples, quinces, and pears when baking or stewing them. The *roots* when boiled are eaten like parsnips with a little melted butter or with white sauce. The young *leaves* go into spring soups, and they give a spicy tang to green salads; they give added flavour to certain green vegetables such as spinach, zucchini, and marrow.

Beetroot in caraway port jelly

Serves: 8-10

1 bunch beetroot
2 teaspoons salt
½ cup sweet port wine
3 tablespoons lemon juice
2 teaspoons honey
1 teaspoon caraway seed
3 rounded teaspoons gelatine

Cut the tops off the beetroot, putting any unblemished leaves aside to use later in salads or in soups. Wash the beets well and place in a saucepan with salt and enough water to cover. Simmer until tender. Peel beets, cut them into dice, circles or quarters and arrange in a dish. Measure 1½ cups of the liquid and return to the saucepan on a low heat with the port, lemon juice, honey and caraway seed, adding more salt if necessary. Pour some of the hot liquid onto the gelatine, stir until clear, pour back into the saucepan and stir again, then cover the cut up beets with the tasty, crimson broth. Cool, then chill in refrigerator until set.

chervíl

(Anthriscus cerefolium) Umbelliferae.
  Annual
Propagation: seeds
Position: semi-shade (winter sun
  if possible)
Soil: average, moist
Height: 30 cm (12 inches)
Part used: leaves

Chervil plants grow to 30 cm (12 inches) high and in appearance they resemble parsley, although the fern-like leaves are smaller and finer, the colour is a brighter green, and the flavour has a mild taste of aniseed. The white flowers, which appear in early summer, grow in small, flat umbels, and the seeds which follow look rather like caraway seeds, only they are a little longer and thinner.

Chervil was taken to various countries by the colonizing Romans, who well knew its worth in food and in medicine. It was valued as a blood purifier, and for this reason it was widely eaten in the spring; it was known to help the kidneys, and was taken to ease rheumatic conditions. Externally, a poultice of the leaves helped disperse swellings and bruises.

This fragrant plant, because of its health-giving properties and pleasant spicy taste, has become a popular herb to use in food. On the Continent, chervil soup has been traditional fare for Holy Thursday, as well as being a favoured dish at other times. Chervil is one of the four fragrant herbs which make up the delicate bouquet, 'fines herbes'.

Chervil's soft leaves make it indispensable for sprinkling, finely chopped, over food as a garnish and a flavouring, indeed it should never be cooked for more than 10-15 minutes, otherwise the fine flavour will be lost.

Chervil is sometimes classed as a biennial, but is best treated as an annual. The seed can be sown in September and March in a well prepared garden bed. Never plant in a seed box, as chervil seedlings are too fragile to transplant. Sow the seed in shallow drills 30 cm (12 inches) apart, cover with soil and firm down with the back of a spade. When the seedlings are big enough to handle, thin them out leaving 10 cm (4 inches) between plants. Keep chervil watered at all times.

This herb is frost-tender, and in cold areas it needs to grow in a sheltered position; it also dislikes hot, dry conditions, so try and protect the plants from the summer sun. A good idea is to grow chervil under a deciduous tree so that it is shaded in summer by the leafy boughs, and yet is also warmed by the winter sun when the branches are bare. As the plants never grow large, it is ideal for cultivation in containers: select a tub or pot 30 cm (12 inches) in diameter, fill with a good, porous potting mixture and scatter the seeds over the surface, press gently down with a flat piece of board, and lightly sprinkle with water. Keep the pot moist, and when the seedlings are 5 cm (2 inches) high, thin them out to 8 cm (3 inches) between plants.

Chervil can be picked at any time of the year. Break the stems off carefully, taking the outside leaves first as with parsley, so that the new centre ones are allowed to grow. If you wish it to self sow, which it will do readily, do not harvest all the plants when in flower: leave a third to go to seed.

The foliage is dried by spreading the sprays out on a wire rack in a cool, airy place away from the light, which will fade the green colour. When brittle, crumble the leaves from the stems and store in airtight containers.

Use: In 'fines herbes' mixture for flavouring and garnishing. On its own in chervil soup and in many types of sauces; in scrambled eggs, omelets, creamed potatoes, cream cheese, salads, and as a filling for sandwiches. Chervil goes with poultry and fish, and is excellent sprinkled on cooked, crisp vegetables with a little melted butter and freshly ground pepper and salt. Whole chervil sprays make an attractive decoration for food.

Chervil soup

Serves: 4
Cooking time: 65-70 minutes

> **500 g (1 lb) potatoes, peeled
>   and diced
> 1 onion, peeled and chopped
> 4 cups chicken stock (may be made
>   with 2 chicken cubes)
> salt and pepper
> 4 tablespoons chopped chervil
> 4 tablespoons thin cream
> a little extra chopped chervil**

Put the potatoes and onion into a saucepan with the stock and simmer with the lid on for 1 hour. Puree the mixture in a blender, or press it through a sieve, and return to the saucepan. Add salt and pepper to taste, fold in the chervil, and allow the soup to simmer on a very low heat for 5-10 minutes. Pour the hot soup into bowls with a tablespoon of cream (or plain yoghurt) and a little chopped chervil on each serving. Brown bread herb sandwiches make an excellent accompaniment.

Brown bread herb sandwiches
(See photograph on page 58)

Fresh, green, finely chopped herbs make delicious and nourishing fillings for sandwiches. Brown, wholemeal or any other health bread is recommended. To help bring out the flavour of the herbs, first spread a thin film of vegemite or cream cheese onto the buttered bread. Pick the herbs, wash them and strip the leaves from the stalks (except for those with soft stems like salad burnet) and chop very finely. Always fill the sandwiches generously with the herbs, slice crusts off the bread, and cut into triangles or squares. These sandwiches can be made in advance, wrapped in plastic or foil, and refrigerated. Serve for morning or afternoon tea, or as accompaniment to soups, entrees, or luncheon and supper dishes. There are no rules about which herbs to use either singly or mixed, it is a matter of individual taste, although it is best not to have too many strong flavours together. Mild, fragrant herbs make a background for a dominant herb.

Sandwich filling:
Pick several sprays each of parsley, chives, marjoram, salad burnet and tarragon, two leaves of eau-de-Cologne mint and one sage leaf. Chop them all together. The dominant herb is tarragon.

chicory

(Cichorium intybus) Compositae.
   Perennial
Propagation: seeds
Position: sunny
Soil: average, well drained
Height: 1.80 m (6 feet)
Part used: leaves, roots (in coffee)

Chicory is one of the taller herbs. The lower leaves are broad and long like spinach leaves, while the higher leaves are smaller and sparser and grow on many branching stalks. The large, daisy-like flowers are pale blue, and grow in clusters of two or three along the stalks; they close about noon, except in dull weather when they stay fully open all day. The leaves have a very bitter taste, and for eating in any quantity, are much more palatable when they have been cultivated by forcing and blanching in the dark.

Chicory was known to the civilizations of the ancient world. Arabian physicians used it, and we know the Romans valued it by the writings of Pliny and others. For many centuries it has been found growing wild in different parts of Europe, and it is known by different names in different countries. The old English name for it was succory; it is also known on the Continent as witloof and Belgian endive. The leaves have excellent medicinal qualities, being helpful to the functions of the liver and gall. Chicory roots when roasted and ground are used as an additive to coffee, or may be packaged on their own as a health beverage, the roots having the same qualities as the leaves. The procedure for drying, roasting, and grinding chicory roots is usually carried out by manufacturers.

For growing in the garden, plant seeds in a prepared bed in September where they are to remain, in drills 25 mm (1 inch) deep and 30 cm (12 inches) apart; keep the ground watered until the shoots appear, and watch for snails and caterpillars.

For blanching, the number of roots required are dug out — this should be possible 6 months after planting, and takes place in the autumn — the foliage is cut off, and the roots are then stood upright close together in a deep box or pot, with a covering of light, sandy soil 15 cm (6 inches) above the top of the roots: they must be kept in a moist dark place such as a glass house or warm shed. As they grow the new young leaves become elongated and blanched, but if there is not enough darkness the foliage turns green and this results in excessive bitterness. As soon as the white leaves show above the soil the plants are ready for lifting, the root is then cut away leaving sufficient at the base to hold the folded leaves together. The chicory now looks like an elongated lettuce heart of creamy coloured leaves, the outside ones measuring approximately 15 cm (6 inches) long. It is important to use the chicory as soon as possible as it deteriorates quickly.

Use: When chicory has been cultivated for blanching, it is classed as a vegetable, and there are many different methods for cooking it. It may also be eaten raw in salads, the texture of the leaves being smooth and fine, and the flavour being just a little on the bitter side. When left to grow wild in the garden, the new young leaves are best to use, as they are not as strong-tasting as the older ones. Tear up a few young leaves and add them to a green salad.

Chicory casserole

Serves: 4
Cooking time: 1½ hours
Oven temperature: 150°C (300°F)

> **4 chicory heads**
> **butter or vegetable margarine**
> **2 teaspoons dried thyme**
> **salt and pepper**

Wash and trim the chicory. Cut it into circles and pack into a buttered casserole dish with the thyme, salt, pepper and pieces of butter between the layers. Put the lid on and bake in a moderate oven, 150°C (300°F) for about 1½ hours.

chives

Chives, Onion: *(Allium schoenoprasum)*
    Liliacea. Perennial
Chives, Garlic: *(A. tuberosum)*
    Liliaceae. Perennial
Propagation: seeds, division of bulbs
Position: sunny, open
Soil: fairly rich, well drained
Height: onion chives, 30 cm (12 inches);
    garlic chives, 60 cm (2 feet)
Part used: leaves

Onion chives when young resemble tufts of fine grass; as they mature the leaves become circular and hollow with a distinct taste of onion. The mauve flowers which appear in summer, are made up of thick knots of cylindrical petals forming round heads like clover blossoms.

Garlic chives, or Chinese chives as they are sometimes called, look very much like onion chives when they are young, but as they mature the leaves become broad and flat, the colour is a light green, and the flavour is characteristic of garlic, only much milder. The flowers begin to bloom in summer in white star-like clusters at the top of long, round stems which are strong and tough, and not suitable for eating.

Onion chives are an excellent standby for giving a subtle flavour to food when onions themselves may be too strong and indigestible, this is because there is not as much sulphur in the composition of chives. Garlic chives are used instead of garlic for the same reason.

All chives can be raised easily from seed in September, when planted in shallow drills in a box containing fine soil. March (or Autumn) sowing is also possible where the winters are mild. When seedlings have passed the stage when they no longer look like delicate grass, plant them out into the garden, or into 15 cm (6 inch) pots for the kitchen window sill. Chives form a small bulb, so when planting them, allow about 12 bulbs to a clump, keeping the clumps 30 cm (12 inches) apart. Both onion and garlic chives are attacked by aphis, which can usually be eliminated, first by watering the leaves, then applying derris dust liberally to the wet foliage; this should be carried out at least twice a week until the pests have gone.

In winter the tops of chives wither back, then in September they begin to shoot again; this is the best time to divide the clumps, making sure they are no larger than 5 cm (2 inches) in diameter: it is very important not to let the bunch of chives get too large as the centre will then die out owing to lack of nourishment. Chives can also disappear if allowed to flower profusely, thereby exhausting the plants, so pick off flower buds as they appear. You will be rewarded with healthy plants if they are watered well, and if a little decayed manure is dug into the soil occasionally.

When gathering chives, do not cut the leaves with scissors, as this causes them to die back slightly leaving an unattractive brown edge — always pick off the leaves with your fingers.

Drying chives in the normal way, either on a wire rack, in bunches, or in the oven, is not satisfactory as they lose their colour and flavour. The chives that one sees in food stores in bottles are dried by the 'freeze dry' method.

Use: There is a classic blend of delicately flavoured herbs known as 'fines herbes' which consists of onion chives, chervil, parsley and tarragon. These herbs are finely chopped and mixed together in equal quantities making a deliciously savoury yet mild blend, to flavour and garnish omelets, cooked chicken and fish, salads, steamed vegetables, soups and mornays. The flavour of both onion and garlic chives is destroyed with long cooking, so if going into hot food, add them during the last 5-10 minutes. Finely chopped chives go into all kinds of salads, egg dishes, cream cheese, fish and poultry mornays, savoury sauces and mayonnaise. Chopped chives make an attractive and tasty garnish.

comfrey

(Symphytum officinale) Boraginaceae.
   Perennial
Propagation: seeds, root division
Position: shady
Soil: average, moist
Height: 1.20 m (4 feet)
Part used: leaves, roots

There are several varieties of comfrey, the most common being the *officinale*, the kind talked about here. Comfrey belongs to the same family as borage, and there is a similarity in their appearance, although the hairs covering comfrey's stalks and foliage are much finer than the rough bristles of borage. Comfrey grows to 1.20 m (4 feet) high, and is a perennial: a thick-set, bushy plant, the outside leaves can measure 60 m (2 feet) long and 20 cm (8 inches) wide. The mauve flowers droop in bell-like clusters at the tip of the plant, and are in bloom for most of the summer.

Comfrey originally came from Europe and Asia. The leaves and roots have long been a country remedy for sprains, bruises and wounds when made into poultices and applied to the affected parts; an infusion of the leaves or roots has been given successfully for chest colds, for the circulation, and for the intestines; the old name of 'knit bone' or 'boneset' was given to comfrey because it helps broken bones to mend more quickly — we have a skiing friend who applied comfrey poultices to a broken limb (he drank the tea as well), and to the astonishment of the doctors, his recovery was hastened by six months. The leaves and roots are rich in mucilage — a glutinous substance — they also contain a beneficial element called allantoin, as well as tannin and some starch. Use the leaves frequently, they are extremely wholesome as a food: the large outside foliage is rather coarse, so pluck only the succulent, young leaves which have a cucumber taste, and a delicious texture.

For propagating, sow seeds in September — and again in March where the climate is temperate — in a well-prepared bed, preferably under spreading trees, keep moist while the seeds are germinating. When plants are a few inches high, thin them out. Watch particularly for snails and caterpillars: even when plants are fully grown, they can shred the leaves to a fine lace very quickly if not controlled. Increasing by root division is carried out in March, leaving at least 60 cm (2 feet) each way when planting: the roots are persistent, and any little piece left in the soil will shoot.

Comfrey roots and leaves should be harvested as required, as they are more effective when fresh. If this is not possible and drying is desired, select unblemished leaves, lay them flat on racks, or on sheets of paper, in an airy place until crisp, then crumble them coarsely and pack into airtight containers. For the roots, dig the required amount for storage, wash, and dry out in an airy place.

Use: Coat young *leaves* in batter and fry them in oil, dust with salt and pepper and serve as a vegetable; gently steam the chopped *leaves* and eat like spinach, or add a few chopped leaves to spinach during cooking; put some *leaves* into the juice extractor together with any vegetable for an extra nutritious drink; make a tea from the fresh or dried *leaves* for coughs, colds and as a general health beverage; the boiled *roots* are made into poultices for bruises and sprains; the *roots* can be shredded and boiled with water and strained, and the concoction taken as a remedy for chest colds — in fact there are many remarkable healing uses for comfrey *roots*.

Comfrey tea
(Using the leaves)

Allow 1 tablespoon of dried leaves to 2 cups of boiling water. Pour the water over the leaves, cover and stand for 30 minutes. Strain the liquid. Drink 1 cup twice a day. Sweeten with honey if wished.

49

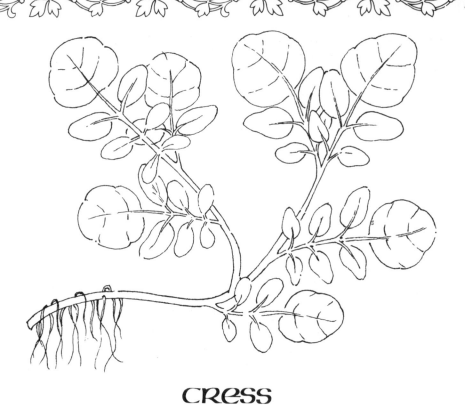

CRESS

Cress, Water: *(Nasturtium officinale)*
   Cruciferae. Perennial (illustrated)
Cress, Land: *(Lepidium sativum)*
   Cruciferae. Annual
Propagation: seeds
Position: semi-shade
Soil: loamy for all cresses. Water
   cress should grow in water.
Height: water cress 45 cm (1½ feet);
   land cress 15 cm (6 inches)
Part used: leaves

Cress is native to Europe and parts of Asia. Water cress is described in an early Anglo-Saxon herbal as being one of nine sacred herbs included in a chant sung by magicians to repel evil, especially the 'loathed flying venom', the song is thought originally to have been a heathen lay of great antiquity. The old name for water cress was 'stime.'

Water cress needs water as well as soil for growing. The water must not be stagnant, so if there is no running stream nearby, try a shallow trough for the water cress. Start by sowing seed in a prepared box, and when the seedlings are big enough transfer to the trough which is half filled with loamy soil. Place the trough under a tap in semi-shade, and as the seedlings grow, gradually fill the trough with water, tipping it away carefully about once a week and refilling with water again. The more the cress is cut the more it will branch, and in summer close cutting will prevent flowering. Water cress has a creeping habit, the stalks are sappy and hollow, the small leaves are almost round with a hot and biting taste. The tiny flowers are white.

There are three types of land cress which are easily grown in the garden, and which we can recommend — their popular names are curled cress, American upland cress and French cress; they are all annuals. Curled cress when growing looks like a fleshy-leaved parsley, the leaves are a light green and the flavour is hot and sharp. Sow the seed in shallow furrows straight into the garden into prepared soil, cover and water well. As germination is rapid the plants are ready for picking within a short time. Curled cress can be sown repeatedly throughout the year; where winters are severe, do not sow once the frosts start. Water the plants in dry weather, and if the soil is poor dig in a little fertilizer from time to time. The best position is in semi-shade, although plants will grow in full sun if they are kept watered.

American upland cress should be cultivated in the same way as curled cress. In appearance the plants are quite different: this type has jaggedly cut green leaves which grow from the centre of the plant in thick, round layers. It is very good value, and will not flower for a year if the leaves are constantly picked. The flavour of this cress is typically hot.

French cress differs again in appearance from the other land cresses mentioned here, although cultivation is identical. The leaves are pale green with a ruffled edge, and their texture is fine. This cress grows in small clumps.

There are commercial packages now on the market containing seeds and trays, which are excellent for growing cress indoors. When grown without soil like this, the cress is ready for cutting before it matures into a fully grown plant. The type of cress used is the choice of the manufacturer of the kit, and is usually accompanied by mustard, its traditional companion.

Use: All varieties are rich in iron, vitamins and trace elements. Cress leaves are invaluable in salads; they are excellent for garnishing; and are delicious in sandwiches. Cress soup or 'pottage' according to Culpeper was: 'A good remedy to cleanse the blood in the spring, and helps head-aches . . .'

Green cress soup

Serves: 4
Cooking time: 1¼ hours (approx.)

**500 g (1 lb) potatoes, peeled and
   diced
2 green outside lettuce leaves,
   chopped
1 onion, peeled and chopped
2½ cups water
2 cups milk
1 cup firmly packed cress leaves,
   any variety, chopped finely
2 teaspoons salt**

Simmer potatoes, lettuce and onion with water in a covered saucepan for 1 hour. Purée soup in a blender or press through a sieve, return to saucepan on a low heat. In a separate pot, heat milk, then stir into purée until thoroughly blended. Add cress and salt, remove from stove and serve. For cold cress soup, chill in refrigerator, pour into cold glasses or bowls, top with a spoonful of sour cream and a cress leaf.

Cress sandwiches
(See photograph on page 57)

Spread very thin slices of bread with butter. Chop any variety of cress leaves finely and lay thickly on the bottom half of each sandwich. Cover with the top slice, cut off the crusts, and cut the sandwiches into squares or triangles.

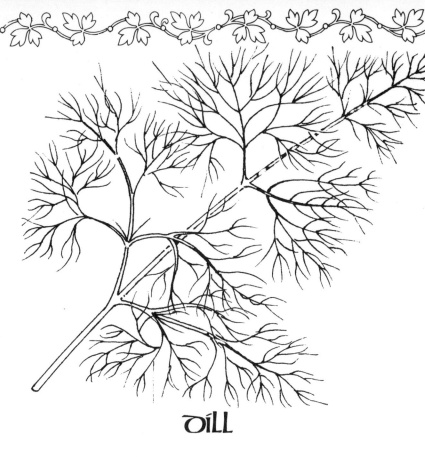

DILL

(Anethum graveolens) Umbelliferae.
   Annual
Propagation: seeds
Position: sunny, sheltered
Soil: light, well drained
Height: 90 cm (3 feet)
Part used: seeds, leaves

Dill is similar to fennel in appearance, although it is a smaller plant. It has plumes of dark green leaves and pale yellow flower-heads which form oval, flat, fruit or seeds, in abundance in late summer and autumn. The slender central stems are easily flattened by strong winds, so it is best grown in a sheltered position, and with as much sun as possible.

Dill is native to the Mediterranean countries and to southern Russia. Its reputation as a soothing herb was well known to the ancient world, particularly to the early Norse peoples of Scandinavia. It was also renowned for warding off evil spells:

'Here holy Vervain, and here Dill,
'Gainst witchcraft much availing.'

The medicinal value of this plant lies in the seeds which are rich in oils with beneficial digestive properties, thus helping with the assimilation of food and dispelling flatulence. In cooking, both the seeds and the leaves with their spicy flavour are used, although the foliage does not possess the same concentration of oil as the seeds.

As dill seedlings are soft and delicate, they do not transplant easily, therefore sow in September and March in a prepared bed where they are to remain. If the soil is sour, lime it well before sowing the seeds in shallow drills 25 cm (10 inches) apart. Firm down the soil after covering, and water well. During the summer, several sowings can be made for a continuous supply of leaves; if picked from the centre the setting of flowers will be delayed. The seeds ripen in autumn, and can be collected as soon as the first few fall. Snip off the heads and spread them out on a tray in the sun for a few days; when completely dry, the seeds shake out easily from the heads; they should then be stored in airtight containers. If wishing to re-sow dill seed, it should be done within three years for good germinating results.

For drying the aromatic anise-tasting foliage, start cutting the leafy stalks before the flower-heads appear to retain maximum flavour, then spread out the frond-like leaves on a wire rack in a shady, cool place. When dry the leaves are rubbed away from their stalks and kept sealed until needed.

Use: Dill *seed* flavours and helps digest steamed cabbage, cole-slaw, sauerkraut, cucumbers, onions, various chutneys and pickles, pastries, breads, sauces, and cooked root vegetables. The finely chopped *leaves* go with almost all foods as their flavour is pleasing to most palates: try mixing a little into cottage or cream cheese; sprinkle some over omelets while cooking; stir a spoonful into white sauce and into salad dressings; use lavishly in green salads; mix through a potato salad, and sprinkle over thinly sliced cucumber; spread quite thickly over lamb, veal, or chicken while roasting, and add a little more to the gravy; dill *leaves* are an excellent flavouring for fish, shellfish, rice and egg dishes; sprinkle them over cooked, buttered vegetables as a tasty garnish, and use in the same way for soup.

Over Blender Borage Soup (see recipe on page 36).
Port Wine and Bergamot Jelly (see recipe on page 33).

Baked broccoli with dill seed and sour cream

Serves: 4
Cooking time: 20-30 minutes
Oven temperature: 180°C (350°F)

500 g (1 lb) broccoli, cooked, or
   1 small cauliflower, cooked
2 teaspoons dill seed
salt and pepper
1 cup sour cream
1 cup breadcrumbs
green dill for garnish

Place cooked broccoli (or cooked cauliflower) in an oven-proof dish. Sprinkle with dill seed, dust with salt and pepper, cover with sour cream, and top with breadcrumbs. Bake in a moderate oven 180°C (350°F) until crumbs are brown. Garnish with a few sprays of green dill if available.

Crab mousse and caviare
(See photograph opposite)

Serves: 4

1¼ cups (½ pint) mayonnaise
1¼ cups (½ pint) cream
2 teaspoons green dill
salt
pinch of cayenne pepper
500 g (1 lb) crab meat
1 tablespoon boiling water
1 dessertspoon gelatine
1½-2 oz red or black caviare
sprays of fresh herbs
lettuce or endive leaves

Blend mayonnaise and cream together in a mixing bowl, add green dill, salt and cayenne pepper. Flake crab meat and fold into the other ingredients. Pour boiling water onto gelatine, stir until clear, combine with crab mixture. Pour into a mould previously rinsed with cold water. Chill in refrigerator until set. Unmould onto a serving plate, place caviare on top of mousse and surround with sprays of fresh herbs, or with salad greens. Serve with Herb Sandwiches (see page 43).

Over Cress Sandwiches (see recipe on page 52).
Crab Mousse and Caviare (see recipe above) and Herb Sandwiches (see recipe on page 43).

fennel, florence

(Foeniculum vulgare dulce) Umbelliferae.
   Annual
Propagation: seeds
Position: sunny
Soil: well drained, medium to light
Height: 90 cm (3 feet)
Part used: swollen stem base, foliage,
   seeds

The fennel mentioned here must not be confused with the wild fennel *(F. vulgare)* which is a tall-growing perennial that does not produce the swollen stem base of the annual variety. Perennial fennel is usually found growing wild in low-lying places that are subject to flooding, and also along road-side banks and ditches. It is often wrongly referred to as aniseed because of a similarity in flavour and appearance, (see page 16 for a description of anise). Florence fennel is recommended for the home gardener because of its many uses in the kitchen: stem base, foliage and seeds all being valuable in different ways.

The foliage is feathery and light green in colour, the bright yellow flower-umbels bloom in summer and are followed in early autumn by seeds of pale green that dry to a light biscuit colour.

Although fennel is a native of the Mediterranean lands, its origins are shrouded in mystical legends, and the wondrous properties of the leaves and especially the seeds, are found in the folklore of many countries. It was certainly one of the good 'magical' herbs, a sure defence against all evil. It has always had the reputation for helping the eyesight (and some say with second-sight also); fennel seed tea is still used by many for bathing sore eyes, the tea also relieves flatulence, and for hundreds of years has been recommended for those who wish to lose weight. Fennel seed can be bought commercially either whole or ground.

Like other similar plants belonging to the same family, anise, caraway, coriander, and dill, fennel's main qualities lie in the etheric oil concentrated in the seeds. Fennel and dill leaves have a similar taste, fennel's being stronger and a little coarser. The swollen stem base is crisp to bite on.

If growing Florence fennel for the swollen stems, sow seed in late spring (November) or early summer (December), straight into the ground where plants are to remain, in rows of shallow drills that are 30 cm (12 inches) apart, the seedlings to be thinned out later to 20 cm (8 inches) apart. The seed bed should be well dug, then limed and manured if necessary; a rich soil will give best results. Autumn sowing in March can be done if the plants are to be grown only for the seed and foliage, but this is too late if wishing to use the thickened stems.

Fennel requires plenty of water during dry periods for a sizeable base, and to give the foliage a good colour. When the base has swollen to the size of a golf ball, cover with earth, continually adding more to keep the bulb covered as it swells. Remove flower heads as they appear. After about 14 days the swollen base or bulb will be large enough to use; cut each one away from the roots and tie together by the foliage and hang in a dry place until required. Florence fennel bulbs are seen hanging like this in greengrocer shops where they are usually referred to as finocchio. It is advisable to use the bulbs within 10 days after cutting, otherwise the fresh, crisp texture is lost.

Unlike dill, the drying of the foliage is not recommended: it is a little too sappy for success, and therefore by the time it has dried most of the flavour has been lost; however, it can be picked and used fresh at any time. If wishing to dry the heads for the seeds, allow them to ripen in autumn, then treat in the same way as dill — that is, clip off the heads, sun-dry for a few days, then shake out all the seeds and store in airtight containers.

Use: Fennel *seeds* either whole or ground, help digest starchy foods like bread, pastries, biscuits and pasta; they assist the assimilation of cabbage, Brussels sprouts, broccoli,

61

cauliflower and onions, as well as many root vegetables. Fennel *seed* tea is helpful for flatulence. Fennel *leaves* can be chopped and used sparingly to flavour and help digest potato salad, green salad, spaghetti sauce and rice; use with fish while cooking — in fact the *leaves* are traditional with fish, and if baking a whole fish, branches of the foliage make a fragrant bed for it to rest on during cooking. The swollen *base* can be cut into thin rings and separated like an onion for salads; or the *base* can be cut in half and cooked as a vegetable and served with a plain white sauce, or with a cheese sauce.

Fennel bulbs with cheese sauce

For a light lunch.
Serves: 4

Trim and wash 2 fennel bulbs, cut in halves and simmer in boiling water for 20 minutes. Drain well, then lay the bulbs cut side down in an ovenproof dish and pour 1 cup of white sauce over them. (Some finely chopped fennel leaves stirred into the sauce first is an excellent addition.) Sprinkle 2 tablespoons of grated tasty cheese over the top and place under the griller until the cheese has melted. Serve hot.

Baked fish flavoured with fennel
(See photograph on page 75)

Serves: 2
Cooking time: 1 hour (approx)
Oven temperature: 180°C (350°F)

> **a bunch of leafy fennel stalks**
> **2 whole cleaned and scaled fish,**
>   **each about 500 g (1 lb)**
> **½ cup vegetable oil**
> **1 sliced lemon, or lime**
> **salt and freshly ground pepper**

Lay the fennel on the bottom of a baking dish, rest the fish on it. With a sharp knife make several cuts down the back of the fish, then insert the slices of lemon into the cuts. Pour oil over the fish, dust with salt and pepper, and cover loosely with brown paper. Place baking dish in a moderate oven, 180°C (350°F) for about 1 hour, or until the fish is cooked, basting from time to time with the pan juices. Remove the brown paper for the last 15 minutes. Do not serve all the fennel with the fish, but allow any particles of leaves adhering to them to remain.

garlic

(Allium sativum) Liliaceae. Perennial
Propagation: segments of bulbs
Position: sunny
Soil: well drained
Height: 90 cm (3 feet)
Part used: bulb

Garlic grows into a tall 90 cm (3 feet) high plant with long, flat leaves measuring approximately 25 mm (1 inch) across and 30 cm (12 inches) long. From the centre of the plant a willowy, round flower-stalk thrusts upwards above the greyish leaves, the flower that appears being a compact collection of mauve-tinted white petals. These blossoms, either fresh or dried, are sometimes used in floral arrangements.

Garlic has been known for so many hundreds of years; its origins are rather obscure: it is thought to have come first from south-eastern Siberia, from whence it spread to the Mediterranean countries where it became naturalized. It was known in antiquity, Homer having mentioned it several times; other classic writers who recorded it were Pliny, Virgil and Horace, and later, Chaucer and Shakespeare. Garlic was included in the diet of the ancient Egyptians, Romans and Greeks, and the knowledge of its excellent qualities circulated down through the centuries, and into different countries. It has remarkable beneficial qualities, and is known to be a natural antiseptic. For this reason, people were bidden to eat it to cleanse the intestines, to help lower high blood-pressure, to expel worms, to ward off colds, to ease chest congestion and to alleviate rheumatism, while the raw juice was put on sterilized swabs during World War I and applied to wounds to prevent them turning septic.

Garlic is indispensable in many types of cooking; not only does it impart its own unique aroma, thus heightening the taste and savour of the dish, but it aids the digestion as well. Before using the bulblets, or cloves, for eating, their transparent skin should be peeled away. There are many who feel that garlic is an acquired taste, and prefer only the merest whiff of the bulb's pungent scent, therefore it is more acceptable for them to rub a salad bowl, a saucepan, or a casserole dish with a cut clove of garlic, rather than to use whole cloves in their food — eventually if, and when, one becomes addicted, the amount of garlic may be increased gradually until the ideal quantity for each person is reached. There are others who can never have enough garlic, and for them one of the most delicious foods is *aioli*, originating from provincial France. It is a thick, strong-tasting, golden mayonnaise made with eggs, olive oil and crushed garlic, to be eaten with peeled, boiled potatoes and mopped up with bread, or to serve together with a bowl of shelled hard-boiled eggs, or to have as a sauce to accompany globe artichokes, avocados, asparagus, boiled fish, steamed chicken, or snails . . . the combinations are many and varied.

Mature garlic bulbs are made up of tightly clustered bulblets or cloves, each being sheathed in a pearly, papery skin, the whole bulb is 'tissue-wrapped' in the same type of covering, which must be removed so that the bulbs can be broken away from each other; for planting purposes do not remove the skin from the cloves themselves. September or March is the best time for growing garlic. Separate the bulblets, and keeping them upright with the root-end downwards, press them into drills 5 cm (2 inches) deep into soil which has previously been dug deeply and thoroughly turned over — with the addition of well-decayed manure if the ground is poor. Keep the cloves 15 cm (6 inches) apart, cover with soil and water well. Soon the spear-like, grey-green leaves appear, then come the flower-stalks, each with a long, swelling bud at the end. As the stalks lengthen and the buds grow plumper, they eventually burst into flower.

Harvesting of the bulbs usually happens about 6 months after planting the cloves, and takes place when the flowers are fading and the leaves are yellowing and beginning to shrivel. Dig the bulbs, shake them free of dirt, and plait several together with the remaining leaves. Hang the plaited garlic in a dry place where air is circulating: if the bulbs are exposed to a moist atmosphere they will mildew. When the bulbs have hardened, any remnants of foliage can be cut away and the knobs stored in a dry and airy container, such as an open-weave basket, until needed.

Use: Garlic is accepted as a universal flavouring, whether in recognizable quantities, or in such discreet amounts that one is not aware of it. It is known in the dishes of the Mediterranean countries. It goes with lamb, pork, veal, beef, tomatoes, eggplant, zucchini, in curries, in Chinese cooking, in salads, certain sauces, in mayonnaise, and in 'garlic bread'. Commercially it is used to flavour salts, and is available in dehydrated flakes, or as a powder.

Aioli

12 garlic cloves, peeled
salt
3 egg yolks
1¾ cups best olive oil
a few drops lemon juice

Mash the garlic cloves to a cream on a board with a little salt, using a sharp knife, then transfer to a bowl. Stir in the egg yolks with a wooden spoon, and when well blended start beating in the oil drop by drop. As the mixture thickens, and when about half the oil has been used, add the rest of the oil a little more quickly, in a steady stream, still beating. Add the lemon juice last. If the aioli separates — and this applies to any mayonnaise — put a fresh yolk in another bowl and slowly add the curdled sauce to it.

Note: Recipe was previously published in Rosemary Hemphill's *Herbs For All Seasons* (Angus and Robertson).

Garlic bread

You will probably have to cut the loaf in half as there are not many ovens long enough to hold an unbroken French loaf. With a sharp knife, cut the bread in slices almost to the bottom, being careful not to sever the slices. Peel and crush garlic, mash thoroughly into the butter. Spread garlic butter generously on both sides of bread slices. Wrap loosely in aluminium foil, place in a hot oven for 10-15 minutes, until bread is crisp and golden. Serve hot, each person tearing off their own slices.
Note: Parsley and other herbs can be added to the basic garlic butter.

horseradish

(*Cochlearia armoracia*) Cruciferae. Perennial
Propagation: root cuttings
Position: shady
Soil: rich, moist
Height: 90 cm (3 feet)
Part used: root

Horseradish has large, dark-green leaves resembling spinach, which under ideal conditions can grow up to 60 cm (2 feet) long. Being soft and fleshy, they are constantly attacked by leaf-eating pests, especially snails. The root system comprises a main or tap root about 30 cm (12 inches) long and 12 mm (½ inch) thick, with several smaller roots branching out from it at different angles. It is white in colour and rather like a radish, but is more hairy and wrinkled.

Like all herbs, horseradish has been known and valued by various groups of the human race through the ages, while today it has a wide and faithful following in different countries. It is thought to have originated in Eastern Europe, and has become part of the diet of many peoples: it was a favourite condiment with vinegar amongst the hard-working country folk in rustic Germany; its reputation spread to England and France, where it became known as *Moutarde des Allemands*. It is a member of the same family as mustard and cress and is rich in sulphur.

Anyone who enjoys the biting taste of grated horseradish will be interested to know that it has a number of beneficial properties as well. It has long been known as a stimulant for many parts of the circulatory system, while having antiseptic qualities too. When taken with rich food it assists digestion, and when a little horseradish is grated into salads and taken regularly it will build up resistance to coughs and colds . . . and these are only some of its contributions to good health.

If you cannot grow your own horseradish, dried horseradish root which has been commercially prepared in the form of small grains, is now available, these swell and reconstitute in liquid giving a good texture. Powdered horseradish root is not recommended as it is weaker in flavour and has no texture.

When planting, select the area required according to the number of plants you wish to grow, allowing 30 cm (12 inches) between plants each way. For instance, if wishing to grow four plants, the area needed will be 60 square cm (2 square feet): measure out a plot of ground this size and dig a hole about 45 cm (1½ feet) deep, spreading some well decayed manure in the bottom before replacing the loose well-broken soil back in the hole. Do this in winter, about one month before planting. In August, after selecting four straight main roots 20 cm (8 inches) long, cut off any side roots and plant in the prepared bed, making a hole 30 cm (12 inches) long and 25 mm (1 inch) wide for each root, and pour a little sand around the sides before covering with soil. Keep plants watered so that the roots do not become coarse.

When the roots are cut for use, soil is scraped away from the side of the plant, and with a knife the small roots are then cut away from the main one, the small roots being the ones used. This can be done at any time. Every two years it is advisable to pull the whole plant out, keeping the long main roots for replanting. The side roots can be stored for some time in dry sand.

Use: A little freshly grated or dried horseradish in spreads, dressings and sauces gives an interesting tang. Horseradish sauce makes a tasty accompaniment to roast, grilled or boiled beef, pork, fish and poultry.

Horseradish sauce

To 1 cup of white sauce add a pinch each of mustard powder, salt and sugar, 2 teaspoons of lemon juice, a tablespoon of cream and 2 tablespoons freshly grated horseradish (or 1 tablespoon of dried horseradish grains). For dried horse-radish, leave 1 hour before using.

marjoram
oregano

Marjoram: *(Origanum majorana)* Labiatae.
  Perennial
Oregano: *(O. vulgare)* Labiatae. Perennial
Propagation: seeds, cuttings
Position: sunny
Soil: average, well-drained
Height: marjoram 45 cm (1½ feet);
  oregano 60 cm (2 feet)
Part used: leaves

These two herbs are so closely related and their cultivation is so similar, that it is not necessary to classify them in separate sections. However, in appearance they are slightly different: marjoram leaves are small, soft and a grey-green colour, while oregano leaves are light green and are much firmer. Their growing habit is also different: marjoram is a compact, upright, shrubby plant while oregano has a dense spreading habit. The flowers of both these herbs are small and white and form tight clusters at the tips of their stems.

The herb we know as oregano is a wild form of marjoram, it is more robust, coarser in texture and stronger in flavour than its gentler cousin, the sweet marjoram of our herb gardens. There are variations of both oregano and marjoram, which are all easy to identify as their scent and leaf texture are characteristic of each strain: oregano is always more piercing in scent, although the leaves of other forms may vary in size and the flowers in colour. The marjoram described here has white tufted flowers on long stems; there is another quite common kind known as knotted marjoram with tiny, white flowers bursting out from tight green 'knots': the aromas are the same.

Botanically, they are all *origanums* , and scholars tell us they first grew in the Mediterranean regions, and were also widely distributed in parts of Asia and North Africa. The Greeks thought very highly of the wild marjoram for medicinal purposes, using it for internal ills such as narcotic poisoning and convulsions, and externally for fomentations to relieve painful swellings and colic. The Greeks call wild marjoram or oregano, *rigani*, and there, as in Italy, it is the very pungent dried flower-tops which are mainly used in cooking.

Marjoram was one of the strewing herbs once used to give houses a pleasant, clean smell, and it was a favourite in sweet bags for the linen cupboard. John Gerard, the sixteenth century herbalist, mentions it as 'marvellous sweet' and 'aromaticall'; another old herbalist says that to smell marjoram frequently keeps a person in good health. Marjoram tea has been recommended for the digestion, headaches, loss of appetite, and as an aid to sound sleep. It is a classic ingredient in traditional mixed herbs.

To propagate these plants by cuttings, take new shoots about 8 cm (3 inches) long in October or November when the young leaves have firmed enough not to wilt when placed in a pot of coarse river sand. When well rooted they can be planted out in pots, or put straight into the ground, leaving at least 30 cm (12 inches) between them. When growing from seed, sow in a prepared seed box in September or March and plant out when the seedlings are 8 cm (3 inches) high.

Both have a tendency to become woody as they get older, so to delay this as long as possible, it is advisable to cut out the old wood at the end of winter before the new spring growth appears. After approximately four years, the plants often become so woody that it is best to replace them.

Both marjoram and oregano should be harvested just before the plants are in full flower in the summer or early autumn. Cut the long stems together with any flower-heads and hang in bunches in a cool, airy place: the leaves tend to fall as they dry, so it is a good idea to enclose the bunches with mosquito net or muslin. When the leaves and flowers are crisp-dry they are very easily stripped by running the thumb and forefinger down the stems. When stored in airtight containers they will stay fresh for many months, and for pungency and flavour they will be almost equal, and sometimes better, than the fresh leaves.

Use: Marjoram's subtle aroma makes it an ideal addition to many herb mixtures as it helps give 'body' and depth without being too dominant. On its own it goes with poultry, fish, egg dishes, vegetable dishes and sauces; into salads, scones, dumplings and clear soups. Oregano's pungency is even stronger when dried, and this herb is a popular ingredient in the tasty regional dishes of many countries: it is used in pasta and rice dishes, in pizzas, moussaka, avocado dip, tomato dishes, meat loaf, rissoles, sauces and dressings, and with zucchini, capsicums and eggplant; it is often sprinkled on beef, lamb and pork before cooking.

Macaroni with sour cream and oregano

Serves: 4-6
Cooking time: 30 minutes
   (approx)
Oven temperature: 180°C (350°F)

> **250 g (8 oz) elbow macaroni**
> **1 cup dairy sour cream**
> **4 eggs, separated**
> **1 tablespoon finely chopped**
>   **oregano**
> **salt and pepper**
> **1 tablespoon black olives,**
>   **pitted and chopped**

Cook and drain macaroni. Combine sour cream and lightly beaten yolks, season with salt and pepper, add macaroni, oregano and olives. Whip whites and fold into mixture. Bake in a greased ovenproof dish in a moderate oven, 180°C (350°F) for approximately 30 minutes. The mixture should not be dry, but slightly soft in the centre.

Tomato and oregano avocado

Serves: 2

> **2 tomatoes, peeled**
> **1 garlic clove, finely chopped**
> **2 teaspoons oregano, chopped**
> **salt and pepper**
> **1 avocado**
> **lemon juice**

Cut up tomatoes and simmer to a purée in a saucepan together with garlic clove, oregano, salt and pepper. Cool purée, then chill. Cut avocado in half, remove stone, sprinkle halves with lemon juice, and fill cavities with the purée.

Note: Prawns folded into this sauce before filling the avocado halves is a tasty variation.

Salmon and marjoram pie

Serves: 4-6
Cooking time: 35-40 minutes
  (approx)
Oven temperature: 180°C (350°F)

4 cups soft breadcrumbs
3 tablespoons butter
3 tablespoons plain flour
3 cups milk
salt and freshly ground pepper
juice of lemon
440 g (14 oz) can flaked salmon
440 g (14 oz) asparagus cuts,
  drained
6 hard boiled eggs, sliced
1 tablespoon finely chopped
  marjoram
1 tablespoon finely chopped
  parsley
2 tablespoons cheese, grated

Breadcrumb Case: Toss 3 cups of soft breadcrumbs in melted butter until well coated. Reserve 1 cup for later, and press the rest firmly into the shape of an ovenproof plate. Brown in a moderate oven, 180°C (350°F) for 5-10 minutes.

Filling: Make a white sauce by melting butter in a saucepan, blend in plain flour, add milk, salt and pepper to taste. Stir until thickened. Add the lemon juice, flaked salmon, drained asparagus cuts, eggs, marjoram and parsley. Pour into crumb case, top with the reserved buttered crumbs and 2 tablespoons of grated cheese. Bake in a moderate oven 180°C (350°F) until heated through and cheese is melted.

Marjoram tea

Take 1 teaspoon of the dried leaves, or 1 tablespoon of coarsely chopped fresh leaves, and pour 1 cup of boiling water over them. Cover and infuse for 3-5 minutes. Strain, and sweeten with honey if desired. Serves: 1 cup.

mint

(*Mentha*) Labiatae. Perennial
Applemint: (*M. rotundifolia*)
Eau-de-Cologne Mint: (*M. piperita citrata*)
Pennyroyal: (*M. pulegium*)
Peppermint: (*M. piperita officinalis*)
Spearmint: (*M. spicata*, or *M. crispa*,
   or *M. viridis*)

Propagation: cuttings, root division
Position: semi-shade to shady
Soil: rich, moist
Height: 30-90 cm (1-3 feet) according
   to variety
Part used: leaves

The mints are a versatile family; there are quite a number
with pronounced different flavours and scents, even though
there is a strong outward resemblance, except for leaf colour,
between them. We have listed five easily available varieties,
although other more rare kinds include watermint, cornmint,
catnip, Japanese peppermint, American wild mint, Egyptian
mint, Corsican mint, woolly mint and European horse mint.
Mints hybridize with each other, which is one of the causes
of the wide diversity of types.

Mint's history goes back to Greek mythology and to biblical
times. It was used widely for health purposes, and was
valued as a strewing herb, both for its perfume and insect

repellent qualities. All varieties have the reputation for preventing milk from curdling.

Mints are usually propagated by root division as the smallest piece will grow; however, if this is not possible, short stem cuttings taken after the new growth has hardened in November, can be put straight into the ground where roots will be formed quickly. They are best grown in rich, moist soil, in semi-shade, but will also grow in poor, sandy soil if the ground is fertilized from time to time. Cut the plants back to ground level in winter. If mint is attacked by rust, the plants must be dug out and burnt, starting again with new stock in a different part of the garden. By the way, mint is not usually propagated by seed because it is very small and difficult to harvest.

Under normal conditions, mints will dry satisfactorily by hanging the leafy stems — cut just before coming into full flower — in bunches in a dry, airy place. Make sure that when the crisp, dried leaves are stripped from their stalks they are kept in airtight containers, as this herb does not keep its full aroma and flavour if exposed to the air for long.

Applemint, as the name suggests, has a strong scent of apples. Growing approximately 30 cm (12 inches) high, it has oval, wrinkled, soft leaves and small white flowers which appear in autumn. Sometimes this variety is called *pineapple mint*, but it is one and the same herb. Another variation is *variegated applemint*, also sometimes called *golden applemint* and *variegated lemon balm*. The reason for the different common names for the same plant comes about through mistaken identification, and after some time the name 'sticks'.

Use: Applemint can be mixed with spearmint for mint sauce; when frying bananas for chicken Maryland roll them first in finely chopped applemint; mix the chopped leaves into fruit salads and fruit jellies; be adventurous and try new flavour combinations with this fresh-tasting herb.

Eau-de-Cologne mint is yet another variety with several names: we have seen it listed both as bergamot mint and orange mint. This type has smooth, green leaves tinged with purple; they are oval in shape and grow up to 8 cm (3 inches) long and 25 mm (1 inch) across, with a strong, sharp perfume. The stems are square (as with all mints), and purple in colour, and the plant may reach a height of 90 cm (3 feet). In autumn it bears flowers typical of all mints, except that these are larger and a deep shade of mauve, making them a pretty addition to mixed posies.

Use: The strong flavour of the chopped leaves is too powerful to use in any quantity, although one chopped leaf added to a mixture of other herbs gives a delicious tang; the whole leaves give off a refreshing scent when sealed into ice cubes and dropped into summer drinks; a bunch of this mint in a jug of water on a hot day seems to help cool the surrounding atmosphere; try a few sprigs to scent a hot bath; and dried leaves make an excellent addition to pot-pourri.

Pennyroyal is another member of the mint family. It has small, shiny green leaves and a strong peppermint scent. It has a creeping habit and for most of the year never grows higher than 25 mm (1 inch) above the ground; because of this it makes a good ground cover in a shady part of the garden. In spring the mauve flowers appear in a series of circlets along 30 cm (12 inches) high stems. When flowering has finished, plants can be cut down with the mower, thus making a lawn that needs no other attention, except for watering in dry weather.

Use: Perhaps a little rank for most tastes, pennyroyal is most useful as a flea repellent: try a few sprigs under a dog's mat. The spires of mauve flowers are also an attractive addition to herb posies.

Peppermint is a most useful plant as it is the herb that yields the true oil of peppermint. Growing to about 60 cm (2 feet) high, it has small pointed green leaves with a purple tint. The scent is so characteristically peppermint that it cannot be mistaken for any other mint.

Use: A tea made from fresh or dried peppermint leaves not only tastes pleasant, but if one is suffering from a heavy cold or indigestion, some relief comes soon after one or two cups. This beverage is also a soothing, relaxing drink, helping to promote sound, natural sleep, especially appreciated by students whose minds may be over-active through prolonged study. It is said that if peppermint tea is taken regularly in autumn and then all through the winter, it helps build up a resistance to colds. As a routine, either start the day with a cup, or have it before going to bed at night. In summer, iced peppermint tea is refreshing, and a quantity can be made and kept in the refrigerator for 1 or 2 days.

Spearmint can either have elongated smooth, bright green leaves, or oval-shaped, crinkly dark green leaves according to the variety — both have the same vital, typical mint scent. The smooth-leaved kind is often called English spearmint and is more difficult to grow than its coarser brother: the scent

Baked Fish flavoured with Fennel (see recipe on page 62).

and flavour is clearer and stronger and the leaves have a finer texture, but it is susceptible to diseases and leaf-eating insects. Either of these mints are the most suitable for culinary purposes, and can be grown in the garden in a moist position, or in a large tub under a dripping tap.

Use: Spearmint either fresh or dried is the variety which gives mint sauce its flavour, as well as being used in mint jelly, mint julep and is customary with green peas; chopped mint goes with hot, buttered new potatoes, with tomatoes, in some egg dishes, in custards and ice cream; a few fresh *leaves* on buttered bread with cream cheese make delicious sandwiches.

Minted honey soufflé

Serves: 4

> ½ **cup clear honey**
> ½ **teaspoon ground coriander seed**
> **spray of spearmint (or ¼ teaspoon**
>   **dried mint)**
> **crystallized mint leaves**
> **4 eggs, separated**
> ½ **cup milk**
> **4 teaspoons gelatine, dissolved**
>   **in hot water**
> ½ **cup cream, whipped**

Place honey and coriander in the top half of a double saucepan over boiling water. Beat yolks and milk together, blend with the honey, using a wooden spoon. Add the sprig of mint, and continue stirring until custard coats the spoon. Remove from heat, add melted gelatine. Cool custard by replacing hot water in the boiler with several changes of cold water, stirring constantly. When cooled, remove mint, and fold in the whipped cream and stiffly beaten egg whites. Turn into a serving bowl and chill in refrigerator. When set, spread whipped cream over the top and decorate with crystallized mint leaves. (See recipe for crystallized flowers on page114.)

Peppermint tea

Serves: 1 cup

Pour 1 cup boiling water onto 1 teaspoon dried peppermint leaves (or 2 teaspoons fresh leaves). Cover and infuse for several minutes. Strain and, if wished, sweeten with honey.
Sangria, a Spanish drink (see recipe on page 89).

Healthy brown rice and mint salad

Serves: 6

2 cups brown rice, cooked
1 cup raw slivered almonds,
   browned in oven
2 medium-size ripe tomatoes,
   peeled and chopped
½ teaspoon salt
1 tablespoon finely chopped onion
   or shallots
2 tablespoons finely chopped mint
4 tablespoons finely chopped
   parsley
4 tablespoons lemon juice
4 tablespoons vegetable oil

Mix all the ingredients together in the order given. Serve.

Baked tomatoes with mint

(See photograph on page 38)

Serves: 2-4
Cooking time: 20 minutes (approx)
Oven temperature: 180°C (350°F)

2 medium-size tomatoes
1 shallot, finely chopped
2 teaspoons finely chopped mint
salt and pepper
pinch of sugar
2 cups breadcrumbs
knob of butter

Cut tomatoes in halves and scoop out centres into a bowl. To the tomato pulp add shallot, mint, salt, pepper and sugar. Stir, then spoon mixture into tomato cases. Top with bread-crumbs and butter. Bake in an oiled ovenproof dish in a moderate oven 180°F (350°F) for approximately 20 minutes.

parsley

Parsley, Curled: *(Petroselinum crispum)*
   Umbelliferae. Biennial
Parsley, Italian: *(P. crispum neapoli-
   tanum)* Umbelliferae. Biennial
Propagation: seeds
Position: sunny
Soil: average, well drained
Height: curled parsley, 25 cm
   (10 inches); Italian parsley,
   45 cm (1½ feet)
Part used: leaves, root sometimes

Curled parsley, as the name suggests, has tightly curled leaves of bright green; some kinds may be more crinkled and tightly curled than others, for instance the triple-curled and moss-curled varieties.

P. crispum is the variety of curled parsley that people usually refer to as parsley, and is the most widely used. The not so familiar Italian parsley has leaves which are not curled, but are deeply cut and serrated like the tops of celery or lovage, the flavour being regarded by many as stronger than curled parsley; however, curled parsley is preferred for garnishing because of its more decorative leaves. There is another variety called Hamburg parsley which has a long, white root like a parsnip, and is mainly grown for these roots which can be cooked and eaten as a vegetable.

It is widely believed that parsley originated in Sardinia, although an early writer says that parsley has the 'curious botanic history that no one can tell what is its native country. Probably the plant has been so altered by cultivation as to have lost all likeness to it's original self.' It occurs in mythology, and was believed to have sprung from the blood of a Greek hero, Archemorous, the forerunner of death. The Greeks crowned the winners at the Isthmian games with parsley chaplets; and warriors fed their chariot horses with the leaves. Grecian gardens were often bordered with parsley.

All parts of the plant — roots, stems, leaves and seeds — are useful and beneficial. The roots were once boiled and eaten as a vegetable, particularly the large Hamburg variety. The stalks of Italian parsley have been blanched and eaten like celery. The foliage of all varieties is rich in iron, and in vitamins which include A, B and C, and the culinary value is well known. An oil extracted from the seeds called Apiol, has medicinal properties. Although nowadays the seeds are not normally used for culinary purposes, there is a story that the ninth century Emperor, Charlemagne, after having tasted a cheese flavoured with parsley seeds, ordered two cases of these cheeses to be sent to him yearly. Parsley tea made from leaves or root assists kidneys, digestion and circulation.

Parsley's taste could be described as fresh and crisp, and perhaps a little earthy, it is also unassertive which makes it complimentary to other herbs in mixtures, for instance it is one of four in a 'fines herbes' blend, the others being chervil, chives and tarragon. A spray of parsley, together with a bay leaf and a spray each of thyme and marjoram, comprises a bouquet garni.

To propagate parsley, sow seed in September or March, in finely dug soil, in drills 30 cm (12 inches) apart where the plants are to grow, thinning out later to approximately 8 cm (3 inches) between plants. Curled parsley is the most difficult type to grow, the seeds taking two weeks to germinate sometimes, during which time the bed *must never* be allowed to dry out, or the seeds will cease germinating. If this has occurred, further watering is of no use, the seeds must be resown and more care taken: covering them with up to 12 mm (½ inch) of soil will help retain moisture in the ground for a longer period. Italian parsley is much easier to grow: 3-4 days after sowing, the seeds will usually germinate, providing they are very lightly covered with soil to not more than 6 mm (¼ inch) in depth, and kept moist.

As parsley is a biennial, to keep it from going to seed during the first year, cut the long flower-stalks as they appear, however, the second year's growth is never as good. We prefer to sow seed each year for strong and healthy plants.

Parsley can be cut for drying at any time, and will keep its green colour and flavour if dried quickly in a warm oven preheated to 120°C (250°F). After turning the oven off, spread out the parsley heads which have been snipped from the stalks, on a large tray or baking dish, and leave in the oven for 15 minutes, turning several times until crisp-dry. Store in airtight containers away from the light.

Use: Parsley *leaves* whether freshly chopped or dried, go into sauces, omelets, scrambled eggs, mashed potatoes, mornays, salads, soups, pasta dishes and vegetable dishes, and with poultry and fish; the fresh curly *sprays* are used for garnishing, and when crisp-fried make a delicious accompaniment for fish; parsley jelly is made from the fresh *leaves*; parsley tea is made from either the fresh or dried *leaves*.

Chicken and parsley pie

Serves: 6-8

2 kg (4 lb) chicken
3 teaspoons salt
bouquet garni, fresh, *or*
2 teaspoons prepared dried
 mixture
3 tablespoons butter or
 vegetable margarine
4 tablespoons plain flour
4 tablespoons finely chopped
 parsley
2 tablespoons finely chopped
 onion
6 hard boiled eggs, sliced
2 cups mashed potato (may be
 packaged instant potato)

Simmer the chicken until tender in enough water to come half-way up the sides of the bird, with salt and bouquet garni. Remove chicken, slice meat away from bones, discard skin. Skim fat off reserved stock, (there should be at least 3 cups, if not top up with water), make a sauce with the butter, flour and stock, then stir in onion and 3 tablespoons of parsley. Put a layer of chicken in an ovenproof dish, then half the eggs and half the sauce, repeat with the same ingredients. Mash 1 tablespoon of parsley into the potato and spread over the top. Heat and serve.

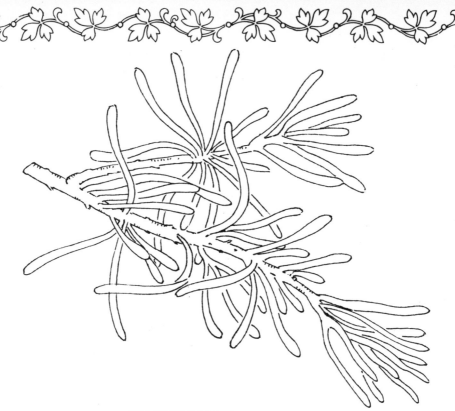

ROSEMARY

Rosemary, Upright: (Rosmarinus
  officinalis) Labiatae. Perennial
Rosemary, Prostrate: *(R. prostrastus)*
  Labiatae. Perennial
Propagation: seeds, cuttings.
  Layering also for prostrate rosemary
Position: sunny, open
Soil: average, well drained
Height: upright rosemary 1.50 m (5 feet),
  prostrate rosemary 30 cm (12 inches)
Part used: leaves

The blossoms and leaves of these two rosemarys are similar
in appearance. Both have the same kind of delicate-blue
flowers, and long, narrow leaves which are dark green on top
and silver-striped underneath. The leaves of upright rosemary
grow to over 25 mm (1 inch) long, while those of the low-
growing or prostrate rosemary are smaller and narrower.
There are several other unusual kinds of rosemary which are
not often seen, including a white flowering variety, one with
gold-edged leaves, and a double flowering type.

The growth habit of the two rosemarys mentioned here are
entirely different: upright rosemary has a stiff, bushy habit,
making it an ideal subject for hedge-work, while prostrate
rosemary is grown more for ornamental purposes as a ground
cover, or to hang decoratively over the edge of retaining

walls. It is excellent in rockeries, and also in tubs, where it will spill towards the ground in a most attractive way. One landscape gardener told us that she had planted a sweep of prostrate rosemary on a sloping bank leading down to a swimming pool, where the blue of the flowers and the blue water seemed to reflect one another. Both varieties start blooming in the autumn, and continue on through the winter until spring.

Rosemary is another aromatic plant which first grew in the warm countries of the Mediterranean region, and it seems to be the upright variety which is referred to historically. It has great beneficial properties which are still highly respected today. One of its main attributes is its association with all functions of the head: not only is it helpful when made into a tea for nervous headaches, but extract of rosemary in shampoos and hair tonics revitalizes the scalp, prevents dandruff, and encourages new and healthy hair growth with a shining lustre — these occurrences having been experienced personally by ourselves and our family. It was also believed that rosemary stimulated the memory, students in ancient Greece having entwined the green sprigs in their hair while studying for examinations . . . this is the origin of the saying 'rosemary for remembrance', the connection having remained with us to this day, even to wearing sprigs of the herb on Anzac day. A few sprays of rosemary, or oil of rosemary, in the morning bath makes a bracing start to the day, but do not have it in the evening before going to bed, substitute lavender for it has sedative qualities. Oil of rosemary also goes into genuine eau-de-cologne, and the flowers and leaves are a fragrant addition to pot-pourri.

To propagate upright rosemary, sow seed in September, or in March where the climate is mild, in a prepared seed box. Plant out when seedlings are 8 cm (3 inches) high, leaving about 60 cm (2 feet) between plants. 15 cm (6 inches) long tip cuttings may also be taken in November, when the soft spring growth has hardened.

The prostrate variety can only be satisfactorily propagated by taking cuttings, using the same method as for upright rosemary, or by layering, which is done by pinning down a stem from the parent plant to the soil, using a piece of U-shaped wire, and covering it with a little soil. When the layered branch has developed a good root system, cut it away from the parent bush and plant out in a sunny position.

Rosemary can be used fresh at any time, the upright variety being the most suitable for culinary purposes as the flavour is better. For drying, cut the branches before the plant begins flowering for the best flavour (shaping the bush at the same time), then hang in bunches in a shady, airy place. When dry, strip the leaves from the stalks. When stored in airtight containers, the flavour will remain intact over a long period.

Use: Rosemary is one of the most strongly pungent plants, the taste and scent of the crushed *leaves* are warmly vital, yet freshly resinous as well: it helps digest rich and starchy food; gives a delicious, savoury tang to beef, lamb, veal, pork, rabbit, goose, duck, and sometimes chicken if it is a highly seasoned dish; is used in liver pate, and in spiced sauces for pasta; it goes well with eggplant, zucchini, lima beans, brussels sprouts and cabbage; it is excellent in herb bread and in scones — try stirring a tablespoon of the finely chopped leaves into your usual plain scone mixture before adding the liquid — the flavour is subtle and piquant, and when freshly buttered and hot from the oven, every morsel quickly disappears. The *flowers* can be candied.

Rosemary zucchini

Serves: 4
Cooking time: 10 minutes (approx)

> **500 g (1 lb) zucchini**
> **1 tomato, peeled and chopped**
> **1 tablespoon finely chopped onion**
> **2 teaspoons finely chopped**
>   **rosemary**
> **salt and pepper**
> **2 tablespoons vegetable oil**

Thinly slice the zucchini and place in a saucepan with tomato, onion, rosemary, salt, pepper and vegetable oil. Cover and simmer gently until soft, stirring frequently in the beginning to prevent the vegetables from sticking.

Rosemary tea

Serves: 1 cup

Put 2 or 3 rosemary tops (with flowers too if wished) in a small teapot, pour 1 cup of boiling water over them, cover and infuse for several minutes. Strain. Sweeten with honey if desired.

sage

(Salvia officinalis) Labiatae. Perennial
Propagation: seeds, cuttings
Position: sunny, elevated
Soil: light, well drained
Height: 90 cm (3 feet)
Part used: leaves

A sage bush in the garden is a most attractive sight as well as being very useful. The aromatic, silver-grey leaves are approximately 8 cm (3 inches) long and 12 mm (½ inch) across; however, when they first appear they are a pale green colour, then as the leaves mature and harden they turn grey. Bees are fond of the purple, lipped flowers which start blooming on long stems in the autumn, and sometimes in spring. Although there are several other varieties of sage, this type is the traditional one used in cooking.

Sage originated in the coastal regions of the Mediterranean countries. It has always been valued for its usefulness as a health-giving and fragrant herb, one of its earliest reputations having been as a preventative against the onslaughts of old age: 'He who would live for aye must eat sage in May' is an old English proverb. It is said to restore energy and a bad memory, and is known to be helpful to the digestion. Sage has long been known to be beneficial for the mouth and throat, and is still included by some manufacturers in mouth washes and gargles. The leaves have also been used for tobacco, for tea, in cheeses and breads, in hair tonics to prevent hair from going grey, and (because of its antiseptic properties) as a strewing herb. It is also a necessary ingredient in mixed herbs, along with thyme and marjoram.

To propagate from seed, sow in September, (in mild climates autumn sowing in March is also possible) in a prepared seed box. When seedlings have reached a height of 10 cm (4 inches) plant them out, leaving 60 cm (2 feet) between each one in a well drained and sunny position that is also elevated if possible. Water well when young. When sage becomes an established plant, water only in dry weather as it will not thrive if conditions are too damp: it is most noticeable that plants with grey leaves do not usually like wet feet or moist conditions. When propagating from cuttings, use 15 cm (6 inch) long, new shoots after the leaves have hardened and become grey; this happens in November, or possibly earlier, according to the season. Plant out when cuttings have developed roots.

Harvest sage for drying just before the plant flowers. Hang the bunches in a cool, airy place. When dry and brittle pull off the leaves and store in airtight containers. It is important when cutting sage, to prune out any dead twigs and branches at the same time, as the plant can become very woody as it grows older.

Use: Sage *leaves* whether fresh or dry, counteract the richness in certain foods while assisting the digestion. Use sage on its own, or with other herbs, when cooking pork, goose, duck, veal and oily fish; in pea soup, bean soup, vegetable soup, onions, eggplant, tomatoes, cheese dishes, egg dishes, rich cream sauces, breads, dumplings and scones. Sage tea is a pleasant and beneficial beverage to take as a tonic for the liver and nerves.

Sage tea
(See photograph on page 93)

Serves: 1 cup

Put 1 teaspoon of dried sage leaves (or 1 tablespoon of coarsely chopped fresh leaves) into a teapot, pour 1 cup boiling water over them, cover and infuse for several minutes. Strain. Sweeten with honey if wished.

Sage mouthwash and gargle

Bring to simmering point 1 cup of milk and 2 teaspoons of dried sage (or 1 tablespoon chopped fresh sage) in a covered saucepan. Turn heat off, cool, strain and use.

Chicken salad

Serves: 2

½ cup natural yoghurt
¼ teaspoon dry mustard
1 teaspoon lemon juice
½ teaspoon garlic salt
dash of pepper
1 tablespoon chopped chives
2 teaspoons chopped sage
1 cup diced cooked chicken
½ green cucumber, peeled and diced
lettuce leaves

In a bowl stir together yoghurt, mustard, lemon juice, garlic salt, pepper, chives and sage. Fold into this mixture cold diced chicken and cucumber. Serve the salad in crisp, curved lettuce leaves.

Sage welsh rarebit

Serves: 2
Cooking time: 20 minutes (approx)

1 tablespoon cornflour
½ cup beer
1 cup grated cheddar cheese
hot buttered toast
1 tablespoon butter
2 teaspoons finely chopped sage
salt and pepper

Blend the cornflour and beer together until smooth, put into a saucepan together with the cheese, butter, sage, salt and pepper. Stir continually over a gentle heat until melted and thickened. Do not overcook. Pour immediately over toast.

salad burnet

(Sanguisorba minor) Rosaceae. Perennial
Propagation: seed
Position: sunny
Soil: average
Height: 30 cm (12 inches)
Part used: leaves

This herb has cucumber-flavoured leaves that are small, round and serrated; they are spaced about 25 mm (1 inch) apart in pairs of 10 or 12 on each side of a slender stem. As the stems become long and heavy they fall outwards from the centre, giving the whole plant a weeping, fern-like appearance. The reddish-pink berry-like flowers appear in summer at the top of long stalks that shoot up from the centre of the plant. As salad burnet scatters many seeds which germinate easily, it is advisable to cut the flower heads off as the stalks begin to lengthen, or it will take over the garden.

Salad burnet is not well-known today, although it is yet another herb highly regarded by the ancients. It is thought to have originated in the Mediterranean regions, even though for a very long time it's natural habitat has been in most of the mountainous areas of Europe, especially where the conditions are moist.

The Greeks steeped the leaves in wine cups and other beverages, for along with borage, it was said to drive away melancholy. Culpeper endorses this by advising that two or three stalks in a cup of claret will 'quicken the spirits' and 'refresh and clear the heart'. It was also recommended for wounds, and was applied both inwardly and outwardly. Salad burnet was often used as a border plant with thyme and mint in Tudor herb gardens.

As it is a soft salad herb and wilts quickly in hot, dry weather, keep the plants well watered at this time. It has no particular soil requirements, is very hardy, and will grow strongly all through the winter.

When propagating, sow the seed in September and March where plants are to remain. Keep the ground moist while the seeds are germinating, and when seedlings are 8 cm (3 inches) high, thin them out to 30 cm (12 inches) apart.
This herb does not dry well, but as the leaves remain green and abundant throughout the year, it does not really matter.

Use: Add *sprays* of salad burnet to a tossed green salad, or use them as a garnish for sandwiches, aspics and any dish for a cold buffet; whole *sprays* may also be added to punches, wine cups, and fruit drinks. When the small *leaves* are pulled from the stalk they make an excellent filling for sandwiches with the addition of a little cream cheese or vegemite.

Sangria

(See photograph on page 76)

This Spanish drink is most refreshing on a very hot day. An added flavour touch is given by steeping a few sprays of salad burnet in the jug after making the drink.

> **1 litre (2½ pints) red wine**
> **100 g (3½ oz) sugar**
> **water to dissolve sugar**
> **¼ litre (1 pint) mineral water**
> **2 peaches**
> **1 banana**
> **1 pear**
> **1 slice melon**
> **2 pieces lemon**
> **2 oranges**
> **a pinch of cinnamon**
> **salad burnet sprays**

Chop the fruit and mix with the wine, sugar and water. Add salad burnet sprays if desired. Serve cold with cubes of ice.

savory

Savory, Winter: *(Satureia montana)*
  Labiatae. Perennial
Savory, Summer: *(S. hortensis)* Labiatae.
  Annual
Propagation: winter savory, cuttings,
  seed; summer savory, seed
Position: sunny
Soil: light, well drained
Height: winter savory 30 cm (12 inches);
  summer savory 60 cm (2 feet)
Part used: leaves

Of these two varieties, winter savory is more popular with home gardeners because it is a perennial. The bush is compact with a rather stiff appearance making it ideal for low hedges to surround small, formal herb beds; if kept neatly clipped it looks most attractive, and was a favourite plant in Tudor days for this purpose, and for outlining knot gardens — in great vogue at that time — as well. The tiny, lipped white flowers bloom in late summer and autumn. The glossy, green leaves are thin and narrow, and are approximately 12 mm (½ inch) long.

The leaves of summer savory are longer and softer and are a bronze-green colour, while the pale pink flowers bloom at the same time as winter savory. The growth habit is different, summer savory has slender erect stems which snap easily, and the flavour is thought by many to be stronger than winter savory, and is therefore more satisfactory for drying. Most commercial growers prefer it for this reason, and also because the seed can be scattered over large areas with good results.

The savories are native to the Mediterranean countries, and their history goes back to the remotest times. Their beneficial properties are strong, and they were once used medicinally for treating colic, flatulence, giddiness and respiratory troubles. In cooking, this herb helps digest many foods, especially leguminous vegetables, in particular all varieties of the bean family — hence it's popular German name of *Bohnen-kraut*, meaning 'bean herb'. The sharp, hot flavour of the leaves has also earned it the name of 'pepper herb', and it is worthwhile noting that it may be used instead of pepper in the diet where this is desirable. Savory is also similar to hyssop both in appearance and flavour, although the colour of the flowers is different.

To propagate winter savory, seed may be sown in September (and again in March in temperate climates) in a prepared seed box, the seedlings to be planted out in a sunny, well drained position when big enough to handle. Another method is to take small tip cuttings of new growth in November when the leaves have hardened, then putting them in a pot of wet sand until root systems have formed. When setting out in the garden, allow 30 cm (12 inches) between plants. If growing savory as a hedge, put closer together, say about 20 cm (8 inches) apart.

Summer savory is propagated by scattering the seed over finely dug soil where plants are to remain. Successive sowings may be started in September and carried on into mid-summer, each crop being harvested just as the flowers begin to appear. When a few inches high, prick out the seedlings to approximately 15 cm (6 inches) between plants.

Both savories can be dried with good results by hanging them in bunches in an airy place. When leaves are crisp-dry, they are easily separated from the stalks by running the thumb and forefinger up and down the stems. Stored in airtight containers, the flavour will remain strong for a long time.

Use: The finely chopped or dried *leaves* go with all kinds of cooked beans either with a little melted butter, or in a cream or white sauce; mix the fresh or dried herb with breadcrumbs for coating fish, pork and veal fillets before frying; it flavours seafood sauces and cocktails, and lentil, pea and bean soups. Use instead of pepper whenever a pepper flavour is needed.

French beans and savory

(See photograph on page 38)

Serves: 4

500 g (1 lb) French beans
½ teaspoon salt
2 teaspoons finely chopped savory
2 teaspoons finely chopped
  shallots or onion
4 tablespoons sour cream

Cook prepared French beans in water until tender. Drain. To the beans in the saucepan add salt, savory, shallots or onion, and sour cream. Steam gently with the lid on until heated through. Serve hot.

Lentil and savory soup

Serves: 4

1 cup green lentils
5 cups water
1 onion, chopped
2 carrots, chopped
1 parsnip, chopped
1 teaspoon salt
sprig of savory
1 tablespoon plain flour
3 teaspoons finely chopped savory

Wash lentils and put in a saucepan with water, onion, carrots, parsnip, salt and a sprig of savory. Simmer until soft. Press the soup through a sieve, or puree in a blender. Return to the saucepan with flour smoothed in a little cold water, and stir until boiling. Add finely chopped savory and serve hot.

Sage Tea (see recipe on page 86).

sorrel, french

(Rumex scutatus) Polygonaceae. Perennial
Propagation: seed, root division.
Position: sun, or semi-shade
Soil: average, light
Height: 45 cm (1½ feet)
Part used: leaves

There are several species of sorrel, most of them are found growing wild, and these kinds are very sour and acid-tasting. The variety known as French sorrel is milder in flavour and is the type cultivated for culinary use.

French sorrel grows in thick clumps like spinach; the broad, oval leaves are approximately 15 cm (6 inches) long and 8 cm (3 inches) wide, and are joined to reddish stems resembling a thin rhubarb. The small, greenish flowers appear near the top, and on either side, of long, scarlet-streaked stalks in summer. As soon as these flower-stalks begin to rise they should be cut off at the base to prevent the plant from going to seed; providing this is done sorrel will continue to flourish for many years.

French sorrel is native to the South of France, Switzerland, Italy and Germany, and is closely related to mountain sorrel, sheep's sorrel, English or garden sorrel, and to the dock

A collection of crafts: pot-pourri, lavender sachets, lavender bottles or cones, scented coathanger and pomander ball (see pages 109-13).

family. Long ago, all these plants were valued salad and pot-herbs, and were once gathered wherever they were found growing wild, to be taken home and put into bubbling stew-pots, or mixed with other green leaves for salads. The leaves were also eaten to assist the kidneys and digestion, they were made into a spring tonic for the blood, and as a cooling drink for fevers. It should be remembered though, that there is some oxalic acid present in the plant, and the leaves should not be eaten too frequently.

Plants can be cultivated by sowing seed in a prepared box in September and March, then when seedlings are big enough to handle, they should be planted out, leaving 15 cm (6 inches) between each one. Alternatively, seed can be sown directly into the ground where the plants are to grow, then thinned out later to 15 cm (6 inches) apart. Root division of the clumps in the autumn is also a satisfactory method of increasing French sorrel.

A small application of manure is beneficial occasionally and Keeping the plants watered in dry weather is a necessity. Watch for snails before they eat away the young, succulent leaves.

The fresh leaves are available throughout the year in moderate climates, so drying should not be necessary. However, if wishing to dry them, place freshly picked, un-blemished leaves flat on a wire rack in a cool, dark place where the air can circulate around them. Store in airtight containers.

Use: Formerly, one of the favourite culinary uses for sorrel was to cook and eat it like spinach, with the addition of well-beaten eggs and butter, or cream, to mellow the sharp flavour, for sorrel on its own can be excessively tart. Another well-known use for French sorrel, still popular today, is in soup. Sorrel sauce is a delicious accompaniment for cold poultry, fish, gelatine moulds, hot boiled potatoes, and as a filling for omelets. The young *leaves* torn into a tossed green salad give a pleasant, appetizing bite.

Note: Sorrel, like spinach, should not be cooked in aluminium.

Sorrel sauce

Makes: 2 cups

1 cup finely chopped sorrel leaves
2 tablespoons butter, or
  vegetable margarine
2 tablespoons plain flour
1¼ cups chicken stock
salt (if desired for taste)
1 egg yolk
1 tablespoon cream

Pick enough young sorrel leaves to fill 1 cup when packed in firmly. Wash leaves and chop finely. Melt butter, or vegetable margarine, in a saucepan, add the sorrel and simmer gently until soft. Add plain flour and stir until smooth. Gradually pour in chicken stock (can be made with a cube) and stir until thickened. Taste for salt. Just before taking off the stove, incorporate one well-beaten egg yolk and the cream into the sauce. Serve hot or cold.

Sorrel soup

Serves: 4
Cooking time: 1¼-1½ hours (approx)

125 g (4 oz) butter or vegetable
  margarine
1 small bunch, 125 g (4 oz)
  sorrel leaves, shredded
8 cups water
500 g (1 lb) potatoes, washed,
  peeled and diced
1-2 teaspoons salt
pepper to taste
2 egg yolks

Melt the butter in a saucepan, stir in the shredded sorrel and simmer until softened. Add water, potatoes, salt and pepper. Bring to the boil, then simmer with the lid on for 1 hour. Press the soup through a sieve, or puree in a blender. Reheat in the saucepan. Blend a little of the hot liquid into the beaten egg yolks, pour into the saucepan of soup and stir well without boiling. Chill. Serve with a spoonful of cream in each bowl and a little chopped parsley. Serve hot in winter.

Note: Recipe was previously published in Rosemary Hemphill's *Herbs For All Seasons* (Angus and Robertson).

tarragon, french

(Artemisia dracunculus) Compositeae.
   Perennial
Propagation: cuttings, root division
Position: sunny, sheltered
Soil: light, well drained
Height: 90 cm (3 feet)
Part used: leaves

French tarragon with its unique, tart flavour and spicy aroma, is one of the most sought after culinary herbs. The leaves are long and narrow and grow on either side of thin, wiry stalks which, together with the main stems, twist and fall in a tangled way, forming a thick, bushy plant 90 cm (3 feet) high. Small, tight, yellowish buds appear in late summer, which never open into full bloom in this country, therefore they do not set seed.

French tarragon is native to the Mediterranean countries, and has long been popular in Continental cookery. Its name tarragon is adapted from the French word *estragon*, meaning 'little dragon': it was believed that it cured the bites and stings of reptiles, venomous insects and mad dogs.

The leaves are said to contain an exceptionally high quantity of warm volatile oils, which is why it was advised to mix them with other herbs and with lettuce, that they may 'temper the coldness' of a salad. Tarragon is one of the four essential ingredients in the 'fines herbes' mixture, the others being chives, chervil and parsley; each of these herbs having their own delicate and individual flavour and texture, which when put together in equal quantities make a delicious and subtle combination. It is interesting to note that of all the *Artemisia* group, tarragon is the only one which has culinary uses; the others, such as wormwood and southernwood are much too bitter to eat, although they have their place among the medicinal herbs.

To obtain a large quantity of new French tarragon plants, propagating by cuttings is advised. Take 15 cm (6 inch) tip cuttings in November when the new, soft leaves have become fairly firm. Insert the cuttings, which have had the lower leaves carefully removed, in a pot of coarse river sand, leaving approximately 5 cm (2 inches) of the cuttings above the sand. Early the following year — say in January or February — the roots should have become well established enough for planting out: allow 30 cm (12 inches) between plants.

Propagating from root division will not yield as many plants, but is satisfactory for a limited number. The plant dies away to ground level in winter, (except in very warm climates) new shoots appearing early in the spring from a creeping root system. At this time, sever pieces of the main root 5 cm (2 inches) long, together with a new shoot, and plant 30 cm (12 inches) apart. By January, these root cuttings will be about 45 cm (1½ feet) high. Although this herb needs well drained soil and a sunny position, it also needs to be kept watered, especially in dry weather. In severely cold climates keep the roots covered in winter with grass clippings or straw.

As tarragon withers away in winter and there are no fresh leaves to pick then, it is important to dry them when they are in abundance. Harvesting may be started in summer just as the flower buds appear, and continued from time to time until May before the leaves begin to turn yellow. Hang the leafy stalks in bunches, or spread them out on wire racks for quicker drying, in a cool, airy place. When dry, strip the leaves from the stalks and store in airtight containers away from the light.

Use: The warming, aromatic fragrance of tarragon complements fish and shellfish, the fresh leaves being especially useful for decorating and flavouring fish moulds; it is an excellent herb to use with chicken, turkey, game, veal, liver, kidneys, egg dishes, and in chicken or fish soups; it can be added to a sour cream dressing, mayonnaise, a melted butter sauce, French dressing, tartare sauce, Bearnaise sauce, and to a green salad. Tarragon steeped in white vinegar gives it a particularly savoury flavour.

Roast tarragon chicken

Serves: 4
Cooking time: 1½ hours
Oven temperature: 190ºC (375ºF)

> **1 x 2 kg (4 lb) chicken**
> **salt and pepper**
> **knob butter**
> **bunch tarragon, or 3 teaspoons**
>   **dried tarragon**
> **4 tablespoons vegetable oil**
> **2 bacon rashers**

Wash chicken and shake salt and pepper into the cavity, add a knob of butter and a bunch of tarragon (or 2 teaspoons of dried tarragon). Place the bird in a baking dish, pour vegetable oil over it, sprinkle with salt and pepper, and put a spray of tarragon, or 1 teaspoon dried tarragon, on top. Place greaseproof paper, or a piece of brown paper over the chicken and put it in a moderately hot oven, 190ºC (375ºF) for 1½ hours. After 20-30 minutes, take the paper off the bird, baste it with the liquid from the dish, then replace paper.

If roasting vegetables, put them into the baking dish now with the chicken. Baste again in another ½ hour. During the last 20 minutes of cooking, remove the paper and cover the breast with bacon rashers. Serve hot with gravy and the roast vegetables.

Tarragon vinegar

Any fragrant, edible leaves can be used for flavouring vinegars, which are made by steeping the fresh leaves in white vinegar until their essence has thoroughly permeated it. If no fresh herbs are available, the dried leaves can be used instead, the quantities being approximately 1 tablespoon of the dried herb to 2½ cups of vinegar. Another method is to heat the vinegar first before pouring onto the leaves.

For tarragon vinegar, pick the leafy stalks on a dry day before the hot sun has drawn out the aromatic oils, and loosely fill a glass jar with them, then pour white vinegar into the jar, completely covering the leaves. Screw on the lid and place the jar in a sunny place so that the warmth of the rays will help to draw out the oils. After two weeks, strain the vinegar into a bottle, and if wished, add a fresh spray of tarragon.

thyme

Thyme, Garden: *(Thymus vulgaris)* Labiatae.
   Perennial
Thyme, Lemon: *(T. citriodorus)* Labiatae.
   Perennial
Propagation: seed, cuttings, root
   division
Position: sunny, well drained
Soil: light, sandy
Height: 23 cm (9 inches) to 30 cm
   (12 inches)
Part used: leaves

Of all the numerous varieties of thyme, garden and lemon thyme are the two kinds which have the most value in cooking. Certain ornamental varieties, like Westmoreland thyme, golden, variegated lemon thyme, and pretty grey Silver Posie may be used in emergencies, but their flavour is not as pungent nor as true. There are also a number of creeping, mat-like species, but they have such interwoven, tiny branches, that the tedious job of trying to disentangle a sufficient quantity for cooking is simply not worthwhile.

The *thymus* family is indigenous to the Mediterranean lands, and is said to grow with more flavour in its native soil than anywhere else. The tiny, pungent leaves have a primitive form, their outward simplicity belying the great beneficial forces within. It is a plant which absorbs sunlight, and converts it into potent volatile oils containing substances that have made this herb a valuable medicine for treating coughs, colds, cramps, colic, the digestion and loss of appetite; the plant also has antiseptic qualities. The special fragrance of the leaves enhances many dishes, and the old, familiar garden thyme is a necessary ingredient in many herb blends such as mixed herbs (the others being sage and marjoram), and in a bouquet garni, with parsley, marjoram and a bay leaf.

Garden thyme has very small greyish-green leaves which are joined to thin stalks projecting in an angular fashion from hard, woody stems that form an erect, bushy plant 30 cm (12 inches) high. The flowers are pinkish-white and appear in spring in whorls at the tips of the branches. The seeds, which are extremely small, can be sown in September and March into a prepared seed box, or they can be scattered straight into finely dug soil, kept moist, and thinned out later to about 15 cm (6 inches) between plants. Propagating by root division is another satisfactory procedure and should be done in September and March: divide the bush into as many pieces as required so long as each piece has some good rootlets attached, and firm them into the ground. Alternatively, garden thyme can be propagated by taking tip cuttings approximately 10 cm (4 inches) long in November, insert them into a pot of sand and keep them watered. This last method ensures good root systems very quickly. Garden thyme, except when young, does not require much watering, and no fertilizing at all. Where soil is too poor for cereal crops, garden thyme will grow well and have more flavour than pampered, manured plants which may look healthy and lush, but will lack pungency. Cut the bushes back hard at the end of flowering, and renew them every two years or so.

Lemon thyme has slightly larger and greener leaves than garden thyme, and the spring-blooming flowers are deep pink. It has a spreading type of habit, and only grows to about 15 cm (6 inches) high. When the foliage is crushed, an unmistakable lemony fragrance overlaying the typical thyme scent is released: this makes it valuable for giving a more subtle flavour to food where required. Propagating this variety from seed is not recommended as the seedlings cannot be guaranteed to be as strongly fragrant as the parent plant; for this reason, the seed is not readily available in commercial quantities. Propagation is either by tip cuttings or root division, using the same methods as for garden thyme. For healthy plants, cut them back after flowering has finished, and start again with fresh plants every two or three years.

For drying both garden and lemon thyme, harvest the leafy branches just before they start to flower for fullest flavour, and gather them on a dry day before midday. Hang in bunches in a shady, airy place, and when crisp-dry, strip off the leaves and seal in airtight containers. The taste and aroma of both these thymes are much more penetrating when dried.

Use: The savory, pungent flavour of *garden thyme* is indispensable for using in soups, stews, casseroles, meat loaf, and rissoles; with all kinds of meat; in stuffings, tasty sauces, marinades, and pate; it gives savour to herb bread and to many vegetables such as eggplant, zucchini, marrow, tomatoes, haricot and lima beans, onions and beetroot. It goes into mixed herbs with marjoram and sage, and into bouquet garni with parsley, marjoram and a bay leaf. *Lemon thyme*, with its milder flavour, is excellent with fish, chicken or turkey mornays, steamed carrots, omelets, and in all kinds of food with a delicate or bland texture. It is sometimes used as an extra ingredient in a 'fines herbes' blend, the others being chervil, chives, parsley and tarragon.

Herbed leg of lamb

This unusual and delicious recipe was given to us by Gretta Anna Teplitzky, a good friend and a gifted cook.

Serves: 6
Cooking time: 3½ hours (approx)
Oven temperature: 160ºC (325ºF)

> **2 kg (4 lb) leg of lamb**
> **salt and pepper**
> **4 cloves garlic, peeled and cut**
>   **into slivers**
> **10 sprigs thyme**
> **10 sprigs rosemary**
> **juice of 2 lemons (optional)**
> **1 cup vegetable oil, or good**
>   **beef fat**

Sprinkle salt and pepper all over the lamb. Make small incisions in the meat with a pointed knife, and press the garlic slivers into them. Place 5 sprigs each of thyme and rosemary in the bottom of a roasting pan and lay the leg on the herbs. Place 5 more sprigs each of thyme and rosemary on top of the lamb, and pour over the lemon juice and the oil. Place in a slow oven 160ºC (325ºF), for about 3½ hours. (The meat should be just pink where it touches the bone.) Remove lamb to a serving platter, decorating it with all the cooked herb sprigs. Pour off the fat from the baking dish, leaving the essence or juice for making gravy in the usual manner. The joint is brought to the table with the herbs on top, but they are pushed to one side when carving, and are not served.

Savoury thyme chicken

Serves: 3-4
Cooking time: 1 hour (approx)
Oven temperature: 180°C (350°F)

750 g (1½ lb) chicken pieces
2 tablespoons vegetable oil
425 g (15 oz) can whole tomatoes
1 small onion, chopped
1 clove garlic, chopped
1 teaspoon dried thyme, *or*
several sprays of fresh thyme
salt and pepper

Arrange the chicken pieces in an ovenproof dish. Pour oil over the chicken, then spread the tomatoes and their juice over the pieces. Top with the onion, garlic, thyme, salt and pepper, and bake in a 180°C (350°F) oven for approximately 1 hour, or until the chicken is cooked, basting it occasionally with the liquid in the dish. Serve hot.

Fish pie with lemon thyme

Serves: 3-4
Cooking time: 10 minutes (approx)
Oven temperature: 180°C (350°F)

3 cups cooked flaked fish
2 teaspoons dried lemon thyme
1 tablespoon finely chopped
  parsley
salt and pepper
1½ cups white sauce
breadcrumbs
butter

Stir the fish, lemon thyme, parsley, and salt and pepper to taste, into the white sauce. Pour into a buttered ovenproof dish, top with breadcrumbs and a few pieces of butter and brown in a 180°C (350°F) oven for about 10 minutes. Serve hot.

confections and crafts

A herb garden supplies us with aromatic and healthful herbs for use in cooking and for making herb teas. It is also a source of inspiration for many and varied scented articles such as traditional lavender bags, lavender 'bottles' or 'cones', lavender fans, lavender-padded coat-hangers, 'sleep' pillows, and pot-pourri (see photograph on page 94). There are delicious confections to make with flowers such as crystallized violets, borage flowers, rose petals and mint leaves; and a host of unusually different items for the store cupboard which include savoury herb-flavoured vinegars, rare conserves of petals, fragrant oils, delectable syrups, and exotic jellies.

Lavender

(Lavandula special) Labiatae. Perennial
English Lavender: *(L. spica,* or
   L. officinalis, or *L. vera)*
French Lavender: *(L. dentata)*
Italian Lavender, or **Spanish Lavender:**
   (L. stoechas)
Propagation: seeds, cuttings
Position: sunny
Soil: light, well drained
Height: English lavender 90 cm (3 feet);
   French lavender 1½ m (5 feet);
   Italian lavender 60 cm (2 feet)
Part used: leaves, flowers

All the lavenders are native to the Mediterranean regions, the variety we call English lavender was not cultivated in England until about 1568. The piercing, exquisite perfume of lavender flowers has a similar reviving effect as smelling salts when inhaled, for it is known that lavender calms the nerves and relaxes tensions. A bath at night impregnated with a few drops of lavender oil sooths and relaxes the peripheral nerves, while lavender flowers in a sedative tea mixture will help to bring on sleep. The leaves, as well as the flowers, have this wondrous effect: notice the next time you are stripping a quantity of dried lavender how drowsy you will become. We have experienced this ourselves, and seen it happen amongst our staff. Lavender also helps to repel moths in drawers and cupboards while imparting its sweet fragrance — who does not respond to the wholesome smell of lavender-perfumed sheets and pillow cases? Lavender is indispensable in pot-pourri mixtures, and in lavender bags and other scented articles. Not only the flowers are used, but the leaves as well: never throw away the foliage, besides being perfumed, it provides valuable bulk when needed.

Among the various types of lavender there are three basic kinds, known individually as English, French and Italian lavender. There are many hybridized versions, some of them quite hardy and successful like *L. allardii*, which is larger than most lavenders and has the long flower spikes and smooth leaves of English lavender, while the foliage has the indented edges of French lavender. There are several strains that have been developed from English lavender; some are dwarf, others have blooms in colours of white, pink or deep purple. The three basic types can be propagated from seed. If a hybrid lavender sets seed which is then planted, the new plants will probably revert back to the original type, so these must be increased by taking cuttings. If starting from seed, do this in September by sowing into shallow drills in prepared seed boxes, and again in March in temperate zones. Tip cuttings of any variety are taken when the soft, new leaves are firm enough not to wilt when they are put into a pot of sand, this is usually in November. When the seedlings are big enough, or when the cuttings have made roots, plant them out in a sunny, well-drained position. This is very important for lavender, as it will not grow sturdily, nor flower well, if planted in a shady or damp place: when lavenders are in a position they like, the difference in the size of the bushes, and the depth of colour in the flowers, is very marked.

Cultivation, propagation, and harvesting is the same for all lavenders. Pruning back after the flowers have finished is also necessary.

English lavender seems to be everyone's favourite variety. It is a bushy, small shrub growing 90 cm (3 feet) high, with silvery, smooth, pointed leaves, and highly perfumed, tiny, mauve flowers which grow at the end of long, spiky stems. When the bush starts blooming in summer it is a beautiful sight, especially if several plants are massed together as a hedge (by the way, this type of planting suits all the lavenders). English lavender is the kind most often used for making lavender articles, and the highest concentration of essential oil is in the flowers. The best time to pick and dry English lavender is before the last flowers on each stalk are fully opened, this is when their oil content is highest. Harvest the stalks on a dry day before the heat of the sun has drawn out the volatile essence, then tie them in bunches and hang in a shady, airy place to dry. When ready, strip the flowers from the stems and store them in airtight containers. When the plants have finished flowering, prune them hard, but not to ground level!

French lavender is the hardiest, and in many ways, the most rewarding of the varieties to grow, it reaches a height of 1½ m (5 feet). The bush blooms continuously for about nine months of the year, especially if mature flower stalks are cut back regularly to where two new shoots are beginning to branch; this helps to keep the bush a good shape while preventing it from having to feed flowers which have passed their peak. These blooms can be dried for pot-pourri and sweet-bags; their perfume, although excellent, is not as potent as the flowers of English lavender. The blooms are pale mauve and grow in a close head at the tip of a long square stalk. French lavender flowers are particularly attractive bunched closely together for posies. The grey leaves are rough and serrated, densely covering the bush, giving it a thick, hazy look. Use them dried in mixtures for pot-pourri and sleep pillows. Leafy and flowering stalks may be cut at any time for drying, providing there is no moisture in the air, and the harvesting is done before midday. Hang in bunches and dry like English lavender. Prune the bushes quite severly when they have finished flowering.

Italian lavender is sometimes known as Spanish lavender, and occasionally, but wrongly, as French lavender. It is a scarcer variety than the others, but is well worth cultivating. This type does not usually grow more than 60 cm (2 feet) high. Although similar to the other lavenders, it is also different enough to make a contrast in the garden. The grey leaves are tiny, smooth, and pointed and grow abundantly all over the bush; we have a curved hedge of 10 bushes growing together at the top of a low embankment, and from mid-winter and on through to early summer they are covered with deep purple flowers that look like smaller versions of French lavender flowers. Both blossoms and leaves of Italian lavender are not as highly perfumed as other lavenders, but the blooms make attractive posies.

Lemon verBena

(Lippia citriodora) Verbenaceae.
   Perennial
Propagation: cuttings
Position: sheltered, sunny
Soil: medium to light

Height: 3-4½ m (10-15 feet)
Part used: leaves, flowers

Lemon verbena originated in Chile, and was introduced to England in 1784. It is a small, deciduous tree, growing no more than about 4½ m (15 feet) high, and is renowned for its highly perfumed foliage which smells refreshingly of lemons. In spring, summer and autumn the tree is covered profusely with long, pointed leaves of light green; in summer the mauve flowerets appear clustered in small plumes at the end of leafy branches. As winter approaches the leaves begin to turn yellow and fall, until by mid-winter the branches are quite bare. When the tree is about three-years-old, it should be pruned back hard every winter, it will then reward you by growing even bigger and better during the warm months.

Lemon verbena leaves are a valuable ingredient in all pot-pourri and sweet bag mixtures; they are especially important in sleep pillows, their fresh, light scent will bring sweet dreams, the Greeks say. Lemon verbena sachets in pale green or lemon are popular amongst young people in some countries instead of lavender sachets.

Propagation is from 15 cm (6 inch) long, pencil-thick hard-wood cuttings taken in winter when the tree is bare. Trim off any side shoots and cut the top at an angle to prevent moisture settling. Press each cutting into a deep pot of sand, leaving one third of the cutting exposed at the top. Water well. When they have made roots, plant in a position where the trees will have shelter from prevailing winds, and yet will receive plenty of sun. Where the winters are severe, protect the roots with a mulch of leaf mould or grass cuttings.

For harvesting the leaves, branches can be cut before midday at any time, particularly during the vigorous growing seasons of summer and early autumn (and flowers which are on the branches are an excellent addition to pot-pourri also), this will help to stop the tree from becoming too leggy as well. The leaves are dried quickly and easily by tying the cut branches together and hanging them in a shady, airy place. When ready, strip off all the foliage and store in covered boxes.

Use: Lemon verbena leaves have their use in the kitchen: fresh or dried they make an excellent herbal tea for reducing fevers, or as a sedative, or for indigestion, and for relieving heat exhaustion in very hot weather. They also flavour baked milk puddings, go into fruit drinks, and are floated in finger bowls.

pot-pourri

(See photograph on page 94)

4 cups rose petals
2 cups scented geranium leaves
2 cups lavender flowers and
  leaves
1 cup lemon verbena leaves
2 tablespoons orris root powder
1 teaspoon rose geranium oil
1 teaspoon lavender oil
1 teaspoon ground cloves
1 tablespoon ground cinnamon
several pieces cinnamon bark
12 whole cloves

Follow the directions for drying the flowers and leaves as described in their sections. Take a wide-topped glass jar, or an earthenware crock (do not use a plastic or aluminium container) and put all the flowers and leaves into it, mingling them together. Put the orris powder, ground cloves and cinnamon into a small bowl and blend, then add the essential oils, combining them into the powder. Add the mixed powder to the dried material in the crock, and with your hands, thoroughly and gently mix all the ingredients together. Cover and leave in the crock for at least one month.

Containers for the finished pot-pourri may be small bowls with lids, or old-fashioned open bowls with no lids, or containers with small holes in them for the perfume to escape. This mixture can also go into 'sweet bags' or, *without* the orris powder, spices and essential oils, into sleep pillows. The perfume mellows with time, becoming more fragrant, if a little fainter, with the years. A warm atmosphere will help draw the fragrance out; shaking the bowl, or stirring the mixture with the hand will also release the perfume. A few more dried flowers and leaves, and some extra drops of essential oil can be added to give extra vitality to a faded mixture.

Lavender pot-pourri

1 cup English lavender flowers
½ cup marjoram leaves
1 tablespoon thyme leaves
1 tablespoon mint leaves
1 tablespoon orris root powder
2 teaspoons ground coriander
¼ teaspoon ground cloves
a few drops lavender oil

Mix the flowers and leaves together. Blend the orris powder, coriander and cloves separately, then stir in the lavender oil and add to the dried material. This mixture may go into sachets or into bowls.

Note: The quantities given are for dried flowers and foliage.

Lavender sachets
(See photograph on page 94)

These can be made in different shapes, from lace-edged hearts to bags tied with ribbon. The sizes may vary from tiny sachets for scattering amongst underclothes or sheets, to larger ones with loops to swing from coat-hangers. Imagination will help you decide on the materials to use, whether of traditional sprigged muslin in pastel shades, or prints in modern, vivid colours, or plain organza in 'sweet-pea' hues of mauve, pink, mist-blue or soft magenta. Dried English lavender flowers are used for filling the sachets, or a pot-pourri mixture for 'sweet bags'.

Lavender Bottle or Cone
(See photograph on page 94)

These attractive natural receptacles for lavender are perennial favourites, and the art of making them has been known in Europe for a very long time. The dried stems of English lavender have the appearance of fine wicker, the interweaving is of narrow ribbon, and the final appearance is cone-shaped. (The following method is adapted from instructions in *Lotions and Potions*.)

Pick long stems of English lavender in full flower before it begins to drop. Take about 30 heads, then with mauve ribbon 3mm (1/8") wide, tie the heads tightly together just below the flower spikes, leaving only one end of ribbon, this should be about 106.5 cm (3½ feet) long. Bend the stems carefully over just below the ribbon knot, and begin interweaving the length of ribbon through alternate stalks, going round and round the stems until the flowers are enclosed. At this point, twist the ribbon several times round the stalks to secure them, knot the ribbon, cut it, and secure with needle and thread. Make a small bow with extra ribbon, and a loop for hanging, and sew to the cone where the ribbon was finished off.

Crystallized flowers and leaves: rose petals, violets, borage flowers, mint leaves; rose petal vinegar (red) and rosemary hair rinse (green) (see page 114).

scented coathanger

(See photograph on page 94)

Make one of the preparations for a sweet sachet or lavender bag and fill a muslin bag the length of a wooden coathanger. Cover the hanger with plain material and sew the filled muslin bag into place on top of the hanger. Cover the hanger completely with a suitable material (silk, organza or sprigged muslin in pastel colours are all pretty). Softly pleat the material and cover the hook too. An extra touch may be added by swinging a sweet sachet by a length of ribbon from the centre of the hanger.

Note: Previously published in Rosemary Hemphill's *Fragrance and Flavour* (Angus and Robertson).

pomander ball

(See photograph on page 94)

Several different kinds of fruit can be used in the making of pomanders, including oranges, lemons, and apples. Whole cloves and ground cinnamon preserve and spice the fruit, powdered orris root helps with the drying. There is one important factor to remember for success, and that is that the fruit be *FRESH*, if not there is a strong chance that mildew will start within one or two weeks after sticking in the cloves. After the cloves have been pressed into the fruit and it has thoroughly dried out and become hard, it will not deteriorate, but will just grow smaller with time.

To make a pomander ball, take the fruit of your choice, making sure that it is fresh and that the skin is thin and unblemished. Measure approximately one cupful of cloves, then press each clove all over the fruit, starting from the stalk end and going round and round until it is covered. For a hanging pomander, now press a staple into the top. Mix together on a square of tissue paper 2 teaspoons orris root powder and 2 teaspoons ground cinnamon. Roll the fruit in this, then twist the paper lightly together round it and store in a dark cupboard for a few weeks. When the pomander has hardened, shake off any excess powder, then thread ribbon through the staple, tie in a loop and finish with a bow. For a change use ground coriander seed instead of cinnamon.

A collection of spices, for details see page 116.

CRYSTALLIZED FLOWERS

(See photograph on page 111)

The following method is the simplest and quickest way to crystallize flowers. Whole small blooms, or single petals may be used, the most suitable being violets, borage flowers, rosemary flowers, English primroses, rose petals and small, whole rosebuds. (The various scented mint leaves are excellent too.)

Put the white of an egg into a saucer, break it up with a fork, but do not whip. Take a dry flower, or a single petal, and with a small paint brush dipped into the egg white, cover it completely, then shake caster sugar through a fine sieve over the flower, first on one side, then the other. As they are finished, spread them out on greaseproof paper laid in a small oven dish. Put the flowers in a very slow oven with the door open for approximately 10-15 minutes, gently turning them as the sugar hardens. Do not leave too long or they will go brown. Store the candied flowers between layers of greaseproof paper in an airtight box.

ROSE PETAL VINEGAR

(See photograph on page 111)

Pull the petals gently from about five red, or deep pink roses and put them into a glass jar. Pour 1½ cups of white vinegar over the petals and screw the lid on to the jar. Infuse on a sunny window shelf for one week, then strain the ruby coloured vinegar into a bottle, and secure the lid. For headaches, pour some of the rose petal vinegar into a bowl and soak a clean cloth in it, wring out and apply to the forehead. Repeat until the vinegar in the bowl is used up.

ROSEMARY HAIR RINSE

(See photograph on page 111)

Pick at least 4-6 sprays of rosemary, put in a saucepan, cover with 3 cups of water, put the lid on and simmer for 15 minutes. Strain, cool, and use as a final rinse for the hair.

spices

True spices, as mentioned in the introduction, come from plants that have a powerful concentration of aromatic essences in one particular part; when dried the aromas are even more intensified. Varying with the plant these parts may be roots, seeds, bark, pods, or stigmas, and are not the leaves as with herbs.

There is a number of blends of true spices on the market, like curry powder, mixed spices and pickling spice. There are also many seasonings classed as spices, which are commercial mixtures with some true spices in their composition, together with synthetic flavourings, and these cover an ever-widening range of complex seasoning combinations.

The gathering, drying and preparation of most spices is specialized work, and nearly all the plants are too exotic to grow in home gardens, so we have given a short biography, as well as suggestions for use, of those familiar, true spices which are easily available and in general use.

For those who would like to make up their own curry blend, mixed spice and pickling spice, we have given a sample recipe of each. All are in small quantities, so that fresh batches can be made when required.

Pickling spice

The following ingredients are for whole spices.

> **2 tablespoons allspice (or pimento)**
> **1 tablespoon black peppercorns**
> **1 tablespoon mustard seed**
> **2 teaspoons fennel seed**
> **2 teaspoons dill seed**
> **2 teaspoons birds-eye chillies**
> **1 teaspoon cloves**
> **2 teaspoons cinnamon bark, broken small**
> **2 tablespoons crushed bay leaves**

Mix the above ingredients together and keep in an airtight jar for freshness. Add these spices as they are, to pickles, chutneys and spiced vinegars, or tie them in a cheesecloth bag and remove later.

Indian curry blend

The following ingredients are for the ground product, so if they are at all lumpy, sieve them before mixing.

> **4 teaspoons coriander**
> **2 teaspoons cumin**
> **2 teaspoons tumeric**
> **1 teaspoon ginger**
> **½ teaspoon chilli**
> **1 teaspoon cinnamon**
> **¼ teaspoon cloves**
> **1 teaspoon fenugreek**
> **¼ teaspoon mustard**
> **¼ teaspoon black pepper**

Blend thoroughly all the above ingredients together. Keep in an airtight jar.

Mixed spice

As these ingredients are for the ground spices, if at all lumpy, sieve them before mixing.

> **5 teaspoons coriander**
> **4 teaspoons cinnamon**
> **1 teaspoon allspice**
> **½ teaspoon nutmeg**
> **½ teaspoon ginger**
> **small pinch cloves**

Thoroughly blend all the above ingredients together. Keep in an airtight jar.

Spice identification for photograph on page 112

Spices in foreground on flat wooden dishes: curry powder, paprika, coriander, tumeric.

In foreground jar: red bird's-eye chillies.

Front row left to right: whole white peppercorns, allspice, mustard seed, black peppercorns, cinnamon bark.

Back row: whole nutmegs, dill seed.

Greenery: fennel in copper jug; parsley in front.

allspice

(Pimenta officinalis) Myrtaceae.
   Perennial
   Part used: berries

Allspice comes from a tall tree which is native to Central America and the West Indies. They are cultivated in Jamaica on a large scale, which is why allspice is sometimes called Jamaica pepper: another name for it is pimento, which can be confusing. The small, round berries when dried are very hard, and their fragrance seems to be a mixture of cinnamon, cloves and nutmeg, which is the reason for its familiar name of allspice. It may be marketed whole, or ground to a powder.

Use: *Ground* allspice flavours cakes, fruit or steamed puddings, stewed fruit, some cooked vegetables like squash, eggplant, beetroot and sweet potatoes; it goes into some meat dishes like meat balls, pot roasts and stews; it flavours some soups and is often used in spicy sauces. It goes into some mixed spice blends, and is often one of the ingredients in a pot-pourri mixture. The *whole* berries may be tied in a muslin bag when making preserves and pickles. They also go into a pickling spice blend.

chilli

(Capsicum frutescens) Solanaceae.
   Perennial
   Part used: fruit

The chilli family is native to the American continent; they produce capsicum-type fruit which varies in size, and in degree of pungency. The tiny, very hot variety known as 'birds-eye' chillies, are dried whole, then they may be sold like this, or ground to a fine powder. In powdered form they are known commercially as 'ground chillies' as being distinct from 'Mexican chilli powder' which is much milder due to other ingredients used to tone down the fierce heat of the blend; like this a far greater quantity than the pure ground chillies is used in a recipe. Cayenne pepper is usually a mixture of several different species of small, hot chillies which have been dried and ground.

Use: Pure *ground* chillies may be used with care like cayenne pepper to sharpen the flavour of cooked and uncooked dishes. It is an ingredient in curry powder. As ground chillies, or as Mexican chilli powder, it is traditional in certain recipes like Boston Baked Beans, Chilli con Carne, and Mexican Guacomole; it flavours chowders, Spanish rice, spicy sauces, meat dishes, poultry dishes, devilled eggs and Welsh rarebit; a little can be sprinkled on certain vegetables like sweet corn, eggplant, onions, tomatoes and carrots. Before using, test the strength of your ground chillies so that you will know how much to use in a recipe.

cinnamon

(Cinnamomum zeylanicum) Lauraceae.
  Perennial
Part used: bark

This spice comes from the bark of a tree native to Ceylon and Malabar. The bark is peeled from long, slender shoots, it then curls into sticks which are sun-dried. The strong, warm aroma comes from the essential oil which is present in the bark. For ground cinnamon, the bark is crushed to a powder. Highly prized since ancient biblical times, cinnamon is still widely used today, and is one of the most popular of all spices. Ground cinnamon is readily obtainable, while cinnamon bark is a little scarcer.

Use: *Whole* cinnamon bark spikes and flavours mulled wine, black coffee and casseroles. *Ground* cinnamon goes into cakes, puddings, biscuits and cinnamon sugar; and it goes with some vegetables and stewed fruit. It is an ingredient in mixed spice, and in curry powder. Both *whole* and *ground* cinnamon are ingredients in pot-pourri blends, and the *ground* is used when preparing pomander balls.

cloves

(Eugenia caryophyllata) Myrtaceae.
  Perennial
Part used: buds

Cloves are hard, dried flower-buds which come from an evergreen tree native to the Molucca Islands. The powerful oil of cloves, which is antiseptic, comes from these buds. The name clove is derived from the Latin word *clavus*, meaning nail, which the clove resembles. For ground cloves, the hard buds are pulverized to a powder. Both whole and ground cloves are found in shops.

Use: *Whole* cloves go into some preserves and pickles, mulled wines, stewed or baked fruit, many meat dishes, soups, casseroles, and stews. They are a traditional decoration for a crumbed leg of ham. One or two cloves in fresh coffee grounds give a subtle taste to percolating coffee. *Whole* cloves are necessary for preserving a fruit pomander. *Ground* cloves go into fruit cakes and puddings, and Christmas mince pies; into some chutneys and pickles; with certain vegetables; into some meat dishes and spicy sauces; and as a flavouring for custards and sweet sauces. They are an ingredient in mixed spice and in pickling spice.

CORIANDER

(Coriandrum sativum) Umbelliferae.
   Annual
Part used: seeds

Coriander is indigenous to southern Europe, but soon grows wild in most countries where it has been introduced; the seed remains fertile for seven years. It is the mature, dried seed which gives us this spice, and the plant from which it comes can be grown by the home gardener. (Cultivate and harvest as for anise on page 17.) The curious thing about coriander is the strange, strong fragrance of the foliage and green fruit. Once the seeds have matured, dried, and hardened the aroma changes to warm and spicy, and it becomes one of the most deliciously perfumed of all spices. Sometimes this herb is known as Chinese parsley. The ripe seeds are slightly oval, small, and a pale fawn colour. When marketed, the seeds are usually ground to a powder, and sometimes they are available in the whole form.

Use: *Whole* coriander seed goes into pickling blends. The *ground* seed flavours fish, poultry and meat dishes; it is a useful spice in cakes, biscuits, pastries and bread; and is delicious sprinkled over apples, pears and peaches while baking. A pinch flavours eggplant, zucchini and capsicums. *Ground* coriander seed is a necessary ingredient when mixing a curry blend or a mixed spice blend. The *leaves* are often used in Egyptian, Mediterranean and Oriental foods.

119

cumin

(Cuminum cyminum) Umbelliferae. Annual
Part used: seeds

Cumin, like coriander, is an annual herb whose ripe seed is the most important part of the plant. These small, brown seeds are intensely pungent, and immediately remind one of the scent of curry powder, which shows their importance in a curry blend. Ground cumin is often an ingredient in Mexican chilli powder as well. Cumin is indigenous to Egypt, and from earliest times has been cultivated in Arabia, India, and the Mediterranean countries, and features in much of the food of these lands. The whole or ground seed is available in some shops.

Use: A sprinkling of the slightly hot *whole* seeds gives a subtle, Eastern character to food; seeds are also sometimes used in pickles and chutney. The *ground* seed in small quantities gives savour to meat casseroles and stews, rissoles and meat loaf; as well as lentil soup and tomato soup, rice salad, Mexican dishes, dried bean dishes, cabbage, eggplant and zucchini.

fenugreek

(Trigonella foenum-graecum) Leguminoseae.
Annual
Part used: seeds

Fenugreek is an indigenous plant of the eastern Mediterranean countries, and is cultivated in India, Egypt and Africa. It is an upright herb growing to about 60 cm (2 feet) high, and is similar in habit to lucerne. About ten to twenty small, three-sided, yellow seeds are contained in narrow, curved pods, and it is these hard seeds with their penetrating and attractively bitter flavour which is the most useful part of the plant, both in cooking and in medicine. Fenugreek tea, which is made from the ground seed, is a pleasant beverage to take, while benefiting the liver and relieving catarrh, amongst other things. The ground seeds are becoming more available, especially from health food shops.

Use: The *ground* seed helps to give a top-grade curry blend its special aroma and flavour, although it is only used in small quantities.

ginger

(Zingiber officinale) Zingiberaceae.
Perennial
Part used: root or rhizome

This plant is native to the tropics of Asia. It is also grown extensively in Africa, India, China and in Australia: the ginger now grown in Buderim, Queensland, is said to be the best in the world. It is the root or rhizome of the plant which is used, and it is marketed in several different ways. It may be dried and then powdered, or it may be cut into pieces while fresh and preserved in syrup, or crystallized. Sometimes 'green' ginger root is available at greengrocer shops. Ginger is known to be an aid to digestion.

Use: Preserved *whole* pieces of syrupy ginger or crystallized ginger together with other preserved fruits, go into fruit cakes and puddings; they make delicious sweetmeats and a flavouring for ice-creams. *Green* ginger is used in some recipes for pickles and chutneys; it goes into Chinese food and into some recipes for ginger beer and ginger wine. If unable to find green ginger root, *ground* ginger can nearly always be substituted. *Ground* ginger flavours ginger snaps, gingerbread, sauces, spice cakes, ice-cream and other desserts; cooked fruit and fruit salad; it flavours some meat dishes and poultry dishes; a sprinkling gives piquancy to cooked vegetables. This *ground* spice is an ingredient in both curry and mixed spice blends.

mustard

(Brassica sinapis) Cruciferae. Annual
Part used: seeds

White mustard *(B. sinapis alba)* is native to Europe, and is called white because the small, round seeds are pale yellow in colour, while the seeds of black mustard *(B. sinapis nigra)* are dark brown to black, are even smaller and are hotter; this type also grows throughout Europe, and parts of Asia and Africa. Although mustard is cultivated mainly for the seeds, the young green leaves are often eaten in salads, or as a vegetable like spinach. Both kinds of mustard seed (and the foliage) have been used in food and medicine from very early times. When the seed is ground to a powder it is known as mustard flour, and it may be bought dry like this, or mixed to a paste with other condiments. Whole white mustard seed is often available in shops, but black mustard seed is not; this is probably because of the appearance.

Use: *Ground* mustard seed helps to give a curry blend its hot pungency, and mustard powder or paste is a universal condiment kept on most pantry shelves. A pinch or more of ground mustard flavours spreads, dips, French dressings, sauces, stuffings, devilled eggs, Welsh rarebit, vegetables, and meat or poultry casseroles. *Ground* mustard is essential in mustard pickles. *Whole* mustard seeds have a nutty texture and just enough heat to be interesting: add a teaspoon or two to white sauce, mayonnaise, potato salad, coleslaw, steamed cabbage, herb butter and savoury spreads. Use in marinades, and when boiling corned beef or pickled pork. The seeds go into chutneys and pickles.

nutmeg

(Myristica fragrans) Myristicaceae.
Perennial
Part used: inner kernel of fruit

The nutmeg is the hard inner kernel of a fruit produced by a 9 m (30 feet) tropical tree which grows in the Molucca Islands, Ceylon, Sumatra and Malaya. It is a spice which has been popular for a long time, having a particular vogue in Europe from about the seventeenth to nineteenth century. Special silver graters of all shapes and sizes were made for the admired nutmeg. The flavour is pungent and rather dry, and does not dominate when mixed with other spices. It has the reputation of assisting the digestion of rich food, and is said to help cure flatulence. These days nutmeg is usually marketed already ground for convenience, although whole nutmegs are also sometimes procurable. One does not need a special grater for them, they can be rubbed against the fine part of an all-purpose kitchen grater quite successfully.

Keep your nutmegs in a screw-top glass jar for freshness. Mace, which is not so easily come by, is also part of the same fruit, being the scarlet, lacy network, or aril, which covers the seed: when dried it is known as mace. It used to be available whole when it was called a 'blade', but as it is very hard and difficult to grind, it is more useful in the powdered form. The colour is golden and the flavour is similar to nutmeg, only more piercingly aromatic, and if mace is stipulated in a recipe and you cannot buy it, most cooks agree that nutmeg will do instead.

Use: Freshly *grated* or ready *ground* nutmeg flavours many different kinds of food. Traditionally it goes on top of egg flips and other milk beverages as a final garnish and flavouring; it spikes liver pate; is the right spice for certain soups like chicken, mushroom, fish, and cream of spinach; should always be shaken over puréed spinach, buttered asparagus, carrots, squash and sweet potatoes; is excellent in cheese dishes and egg dishes, cream sauces, and pumpkin pie; enhances a fish or chicken mornay; and goes into all kinds of spice cakes, biscuits, custards, stewed fruit and fruit salads; and it also goes into some meat dishes. Commercially it is an ingredient in a mixed spice blend.

papRika

(Capsicum annum) Solanaceae. Perennial
Part used: fruit

Paprika is the product of dried and ground ripe capsicums which come from plants belonging to the same family as the chilli, and which are also native to America. Instead of bearing small, hot-tasting fruit, these plants produce large, aromatic fruit, varying in degrees of pungency, but are never hot. For paprika, several varieties of this type are blended together to achieve the best flavour and red colour possible. The plants are grown in many countries today, the best quality comes from Hungary, and is known as 'Noble Sweet'. Another name for paprika is 'Grains of Paradise'. This spice is readily obtainable in shops.

Use: Traditional of course in Hungarian goulash and paprika chicken, where it is used in large quantities to flavour and colour the dishes a rich rosy red; in smaller quantities it flavours dishes containing crab, chicken, eggs or cheese; it is an attractive and tasty garnish for all kinds of food including rice dishes, baked potatoes, hors-d'oeuvre, salads, and cooked vegetables; it can be mixed into white sauce and mayonnaise. Commercially it is a popular flavouring and colouring agent in many savoury blends.

pepper

(Piper nigrum) Piperaceae. Perennial
Part used: berries

Black and white peppercorns are the fruit of a climbing vine, which when left untrained reaches a height of 6 m (20 feet) or more, but for commercial growing, it is limited to 3.6 m (12 feet). It is native to the East Indies, and is also cultivated in India, Thailand and New Guinea. For black peppercorns, the red, unripe berries are picked, then dried with their outer skin intact. Like this their appearance is dark-brown to black, and wrinkled, and their flavour is hot and aromatic. For white peppercorns, the berries are picked when they are ripe, the outside skin is then removed leaving the smooth, light-coloured core which, although hot, has less aroma than black pepper. Both black and white pepper have more pungency and flavour when freshly ground from a peppermill. Finely ground pepper, whole peppercorns and 'cracked' peppercorns are available in shops. Sometimes black and white are found mixed together: they are then often known as mignonette pepper.

Use: Pepper, whether black or white, is a universal flavouring. *Ground* black pepper is a vital ingredient in a curry blend. The purists say that white *ground* pepper should be used for bland, white or pale food so as not to discolour it with the dark specks of black pepper, and that it should also go into pepper shakers for the table, while black pepper is meant for coarser food. However, black pepper freshly ground from a mill has become a popular spice for all food, either while being prepared or at table. *Whole*, or *cracked* peppercorns are used lavishly for pepper steak; used *whole* they go into soups, casseroles, and stews; they flavour marinades and spicy vinegars, and are an important ingredient in pickling spice blends.

turmeric

(Curcuma longa) Zingiberaceae. Perennial
Part used: root or rhizome

Turmeric is a member of the ginger family native to parts of Asia, and is also cultivated in India, Java and tropical Africa.

The root is washed, dried and ground to a bright yellow powder, which has a pungently warm and bitter aroma and taste. In the East, this spice is used as a dye for materials; in fact it should be handled carefully at all times, as even a small amount will stain clothes and fingers. It is marketed already ground to a powder.

Use: The warm fragrance and yellow colour of this spice makes it a favourite ingredient in pickles and chutney. It is a component of curry blends, the quantity varying according to choice: it gives the otherwise brownish mixture a richer and brighter colour, as well as adding to the flavour-bouquet of the other aromatic spices. It is often added to commercial mustard for its colour. Put a pinch in the water when boiling rice for serving with curry. Turmeric colours and flavours fish kedgeree, devilled eggs, fish stews, white sauce, mayonnaise and salad dressings.

vanilla

(Vanilla planifolia) Orchidaceae. Perennial
Part used: pod or bean

This beautiful orchid is another plant native to America. It produces a long pod or bean, which is black and shiny when dried. It has an intensely aromatic scent which is much richer and sweeter than that of synthetic vanilla essence. Whole vanilla pods are marketed in screw-top jars to preserve their flavour.

Use: A piece of vanilla pod 5 cm (2 inches) long should be cut, slit down the middle and used when making special, rich custard ice-creams, custards, and milk puddings, and infused in warm milk for cake mixtures. The piece can be quickly rinsed afterwards and used two or three times. Store the cut piece in a small jar of sugar. Vanilla sugar is easily made if you have a blender. Put 1 cup of sugar and half a vanilla pod, cut up roughly, into the blender, then set on high for a few seconds, or until the pod has been rendered down to black spots suspended in the sugar. Use for flavouring when cooking cakes, puddings and custards, and for sprinkling on any suitable dessert.

oven temperature guíoe

This is an approximate guide only. Different makes of stoves vary and even the same make of stove can give slightly different individual results at the same temperature. If in doubt with your particular stove, do refer to your own manufacturer's temperature chart. It is impossible in a general book to be exact for every stove, but the following is a good average guide in every case.

Description of Oven	Thermostat Setting		
	°F		°C
	Automatic Electric	Gas	
Cool	200	200	90
Very slow	250	250	120
Slow	300-325	300	150-160
Moderately slow	325-350	325	160-170
Moderate	350-375	350	170-190
Moderately hot	375-400	375	190-200
Hot	400-450	400	200-230
Very hot	450-500	450	230-260

GUIDE TO WEIGHTS AND MEASURES

At the time of publication, the kitchen measures used throughout this book refer to those adopted by The Standards Association of Australia (AS 1325: 1972) which replaces all earlier standards. All spoon measurements are level unless otherwise stated. A good set of scales, a graduated Australian Standard measuring cup and a set of Australian Standard measuring spoons will be most helpful. These are available at leading hardware stores.

The Australian Standard measuring cup has a capacity of 8 fluid ounces.
The Australian Standard tablespoon has a capacity of 20 millilitres.
The Australian Standard teaspoon has a capacity of 5 millilitres.
The British imperial pint (used in Australia) has a volume of 20 fluid ounces.

Coates, Peter, *Roses* (Weidenfeld and Nicolson, London, 1962).

Culpeper, Nicholas, *Culpeper's Complete Herbal* (W. Foulsham and Co Ltd, London).

David, Elizabeth, *Spices, Salt and Aromatics in the English Kitchen* (Penguin Books, Harmondsworth, 1970).

David, Elizabeth, *Summer Cooking* (Penguin Books, Harmondsworth, 1965).

Geuter, Maria, *Herbs in Nutrition* (Bio-Dynamic Agricultural Association, London, 1962).

Grieve, Mrs. M., *A Modern Herbal* 2 vols. Edited by Mrs. C. F. Leyel (Hafner Publishing Co, New York, 1959).

Hall, Dorothy, *The Book of Herbs* (Angus and Robertson Pty Ltd, Sydney, 1972).

Harmsworth's Universal Encyclopedia (Educational Book Co Ltd, London).

Hemphill, Rosemary, *Herbs and Spices* (Penguin Books, Harmondsworth, 1966).

Hemphill, Rosemary, *Herbs for All Seasons* (Angus and Robertson Pty Ltd, Sydney, 1972).

Janes, E. R., *Growing Vegetables for Show* (Penguin Books, Harmondsworth, 1956).

Leyel, Mrs. C. F., and Harley, Olga, *The Gentle Art of Cookery* (Chatto and Windus, London, 1925).

Loewenfeld, Claire, *Herb Gardening* (Garden Book Club, London, 1964).

Lotions and Potions (Compiled by the National Federation of Women's Institutes, England, 1956, printed by Novello and Co Ltd).

Miloradovich, Milo, *The Art of Cooking with Herbs and Spices* (Doubleday and Co, Inc New York, 1950).

Philbrick, Helen, and Greeg, Richard B., *Companion Plants* (Stuart and Watkins, London 1967).

Ranson, Florence, *British Herbs* (Penguin Books, Harmondsworth, 1949).

Rohde, Eleanour Sinclair, *A Garden of Herbs* (Medici Society, London).

Rohde, Eleanour Sinclair, *The Old English Herbals* (Longmans, Green and Co, London, 1922).

Rohde, Eleanour Sinclair, *Shakespeare's Wild Flowers* (Medici Society, London, 1963).

Sunset Books, *How to Grow Herbs* (Lane Books, Menlo Park, California, 1972).

Webster, Helen Noyes, *Herbs* (Charles T. Branfor Co, Boston, 1947).

index